Peace & Happy

♡

Jamie

Peace & Happy

♡

Love

MY
PEACE
OF
HAPPY

A SELF-LOVE JOURNEY TO HAPPINESS,
PURPOSE AND LIFESTYLE SUCCESS

JAMIE WATKINS

Paperback ISBN: 978-1-63616-062-7
Ebook ISBN: 978-1-63616-063-4

Published By Opportune Independent Publishing Co.
Best-Selling Author Coach: Nikkie Pryce
Photography by Touch of Hart Photography
Book Cover Design by Live Life Creative

Printed in the United States of America
For permission requests, email the publisher with the subject line as "Attention: Permissions Coordinator" to the email address below:

info@opportunepublishing.com
www. opportunepublishing.com

DEDICATION

I dedicate this book to my parents, Joe and Jean Laughlin. Thank you dad for teaching me what real love looks like, the importance of family and the joy of laughter. Thank you mom for always covering me in prayer and being such a steady example of strength and resilience. I'm eternally grateful to God for you both!

CONTENTS

ACKNOWLEDGMENTS

To my Father in Heaven, God, I thank you for Jesus and for being Who You are. Thank you for gifting me everything I need to fulfill Your purpose for my life. I am forever grateful for Your unfailing love, grace and favor.

Thank you to my heart, Ricky. You are a constant reminder of God's grace and goodness. I am so thankful to you for your friendship, patience, support and encouragement. You never let me forget who and Whose I am. I love you 4EVERMORE!

To my children Jordan, Ricky, Kyle and Shane, you've shown me how deep I can love. I love each of you for your individual greatness! Thank you for understanding how important this journey is to me and never questioning why I needed quiet or stayed up so late. Every like, every edit, every hug and every laugh made it easier. I hope that through my example, you know you are enough, equipped and purposed to impact the world with your gifts!

To my sisters and brother, the ones here and that have passed on, I love you without limits, and no words can express the impact each of you has had in my life. I appreciate every ounce of love, support, prayer and lessons learned along the way. I love you most!

To my family, my tribe, my day ones and new ones! Thank you, thank you, thank you for cheering me on, calling me out and supporting me along the way. We grow better together!

To my coaches, Danté, Kelly J and Nikkie. It was by divine appointment that our paths crossed. Thank you each for seeing in me what I didn't always have the courage to see in myself. Thank you for believing in me and always reminding me that

I CAN TOTALLY DO THIS!

To my My Peace of Happy community, you continue to give me a reason to show up! Thank you for appreciating my gifts and allowing me to just be ME. We're just getting started!

INTRODUCTION

Hey Sis, I'm sorry it took so long for us to meet like this. I'm sorry I sat on the vision God gave me for this book for so long. I know now I delayed my breakthrough, and I may have delayed yours too. You may have needed to know sooner that your story matters and that you are enough, equipped and empowered for purpose! Forgive me for sitting on the gifts that were given to me to share with you. We're here now, and I have to believe that it's not too late and that God has designed it that my delay in obedience will not prevent you from everything He has for you. As a matter of fact, I pray this will meet you right where you are and right on time!

I am so grateful you are sharing this space with me. Peace and Happy, two things everyone wants, even if they are scared to admit it. Self-love and purpose, two things everyone needs, although they may not know it. If you are reading this book, you are my person; it has been designed for us to cross paths. When I received the vision for this book, it was simply that my story mattered, and I could see myself at a book signing. I had no idea the transformational journey God designed to take place within my writing process. This book was written for both of us. I need you to do me a favor. I need you to forget what you think you know about me, about happy, or even what you think you know of my story. Walk with me through my journey from happily ever after to lifestyle success. Look for the lessons that you can benefit from to help you better navigate your own journey. Check any bags you have at the door to free yourself up to relax and embrace the ride. I can tell you now that it is a bumpy one, but I hope that some of the lessons I have learned, especially the hard ones, help to smooth out yours.

PART I

How It Started

1

HAPPILY EVER AFTER

Like a lot of little girls, I wished for happily ever after. I am the baby of five, and growing up, seeing how much my dad loved my mom had me set my heart on having a husband that loved me that same way. It would be this great expectation that would set me up for major disappointment later in life. My dad loved hard and out loud. While there is no question that it truly was my mom, he had a way of making all of us feel like we were his favorite. Our home was filled with lots of love and laughter. My dad was the jokester/prankster type, and when he laughed, it warmed both his heart and those around him, even when the laugh was at your expense. "Laughter keeps your heart warm." he said. Growing up, I remember always feeling safe, protected, cared for, valued and loved. I'm a daddy's girl through and through. I could not wait for him to walk me down the aisle like he had my three older sisters on their wedding day.

A big moment in every girl's life, it wasn't the aisle I looked most forward to, though. It was the father-daughter dance. On the way home, on the evening of my bridal shower, I stopped by my parent's house and sat at the kitchen table with my dad. I shared all about how nice a job my sisters had done planning out the shower and hosting. I filled him in on who was there and let him know I had received so many nice gifts. I also shared that in all the excitement, I kept feeling like something was off, missing. It had been him. I'm absolutely certain I would have been horrified opening all those sets of Victoria Secrets with him in the room, but it still felt like he should have been there. It was a big event, a special moment, and he'd been a part of every other one in my life. I assured him that I was comforted by the fact that we would have our time at the wedding, just us in the middle of the dance floor for the father-daughter dance. I know that blessed his heart.

My daddy died suddenly on a Tuesday night, four months before my wedding. Complications from Emphysema, a diagnosis he had kept secret. The thought of him bearing that burden alone still saddens me, but that is who he was. I never saw my father smoke, but from the pictures in the photo albums, I knew he had for most of his life. That decision had caught up to him and killed him. I can remember getting the phone call that daddy was on his way to the ER and to come quickly. Between my sisters and I, I lived the furthest away, having just a month earlier moved into my first apartment. I immediately went to God in prayer, and while I was expecting peace or calm that would let me know he would be ok, my answer came quick and was crystal clear, THIS WAS IT. It was so definitive that all I could pray was just let me see him first, "Let me get there before you take him, God. I want to say goodbye."

I wanted to let him know it was ok that he wouldn't be there for my wedding, that we'd never have our dance. I knew that would be weighing heavy on him. I knew if there was any fight in him, it would be for him to be there for that moment. The longest twenty minutes of my life, I stayed in God's ear repeating that request, "Just let me see him first." Every time I received the same finite answer, THIS IS IT. "I know, I heard you, I'm just asking You to let me see him first!" I didn't feel like that was too much to ask. I wasn't trying to argue for him to stay or deny what the Spirit had made so clear.

I drove as fast as I could down the highway and side streets to get there in time. I am absolutely certain I ran some red lights because I don't ever remember stopping. I had decided that any cop who tried to pull me over would have to follow me to my father's bedside. I pulled onto the hospital's street and saw my sisters and cousin outside the emergency room entrance. They were waiting for me. Only when they saw me, my sisters turned away. They sent my cousin to break the news, and once he started walking my way, I knew. A moment of rage flooded me, "DAMMIT, I JUST WANTED TO SEE HIM, YOU COULD HAVE LET ME SAY GOODBYE!!!"

That rage was quickly followed by sorrow and pain so deep only God could comfort. I couldn't stay mad at Him when He was the only one that could stop my heart from swelling out of my chest. I felt so much pressure, like it was going to physically burst. It was such agonizing pain. Just like I'd heard, THIS WAS IT. My daddy was gone. None of my sisters had made it in time to see him. My mom would be the last, seeing him fall backward onto the floor in my old bedroom, which they'd not hesitated to turn into her home office as soon as I moved out. She would try CPR, but it would do nothing to bring him back.

I can remember my bed, the covers and the pain. I remember reminding God that He said He wouldn't give me more than I could bear. I assured Him that this pain would be what killed me if He didn't take it away. True to His Word and the loving God He is, He did.

Three months later, one month before my wedding day, while on a business trip to Boston, my daddy would visit me in a dream, and we had our father-daughter dance. In the dream, I was aware I was dreaming and aware that my dad had died. I cried on his shoulder, he rubbed my back with his signature daddy pats, and we danced. God had heard me. My daddy had gotten to come back so we could have our dance and so that I could say goodbye. Great is God's faithfulness.

Dear Daddy,

I love you with an unmeasurable love. Thank you for everything you were to me here on earth and everything you continue to be me in spirit. Thank you for your enormous love, for instilling in me a strong sense of family, teaching me how to warm my heart with laughter and how to find joy in the little things. You were consistent and true to who you were. Thank you for that example. I can still hear your laugh and feel your love. I miss you! I imagine how much my children would adore you and the long engaging conversations you and Ricky would have. Thank you, daddy, for giving of yourself so freely to our family. I am forever thankful for the blessing you are to my life, still!

Forever Joe's Baby Girl,
Jamie

Though I have never felt pain like the pain of losing my dad, the sorrow of death was not new to me. I lost my only brother to a car accident when I was nine-years-old. He was twenty-one. I miss him. I remember being confused and wanting him to come back, and that he never did. I also remember being shut in my parent's room when my sister, who had spent the night out, arrived home to hear the news. She'd been with my brother the night before at a party but went home with a friend. I watched through the window at her scream and cry, as they carried her in. I cried out, "I want my brother back!" over and over. They told me he was in heaven. My uncle would explain, "God only picks the best flowers from His garden." My brother would never be there again to get my bike out of the garage, "brainwash" me by singing a song or eat peanut butter and jelly sandwiches with me while watching G.I. Joe and Thunder Cats.

After my brother died, I knew a few things to be absolutely true:

1. Someone could walk out the door one night alive, die

and never come back.

2. You should always say I love you to the people you love.

3. To always lock the car doors and wear your seatbelt (this was before it was the law), I obsessed over it.

At nine years old, his death had stolen my sense of security, and I desperately needed it back. It turns out my brother was wearing his seatbelt. It was just no match for the telephone pole his best friend hit that night when he fell asleep at the wheel. My brother was killed on impact, a fact I would find a little bit of comfort in, knowing he didn't suffer.

It was at this time I created my list of things I want to experience before I die. Yep, a bucket list at age nine because it was clear to me that tomorrow wasn't promised and even if you lived to see tomorrow, you just never knew. I'd learn later this was a form of PTSD, but for the next 20+ years, it would just be my life.

1. Graduate High School.

2. Get married.

3. Buy a house.

Eventually, I would want kids, but I would be just fine being the cool auntie for years, which I already was by the age of three when my oldest sister Pearl, eighteen years senior, had my first niece. Considering my life could end as early as twenty-one as my brothers had, I was serious about what I wanted. I couldn't put my life in harm's way. I was very aware that things happen and people die. I kept thinking, I can't be the reason my parents lose another child. I had watched how sad that made them both. I suppose I did miss out on a little of the carefreeness of a typical childhood. Recently, I heard my mom say that in a podcast interview, and it hadn't struck me till then how the trauma of death had manifested in my life growing up.

Though the sad things stand out, I have a lot of fun memories of growing up too! I was an 80's/90's kid. A latch-key, hot dogs and grilled cheese kinda kid. I played and rode my bike outside till the street lights came on. My friends and I played "house," Four Squares and jumped rope. I caught lightning bugs and ran for the ice cream truck. I remember biker shorts, leg warmers and teased ponytails. I also remember baggy jeans, Starter pullovers and Reebox Classics. Most of all, I remember the music and the nostalgia that comes back when I hear a song from the soundtrack of my life.

My first little 12' single was 'Pass the Duchie', by Musical Youth. Wouldn't recommend giving a five-year-old a song about passing around a blunt now, but hey, it was catchy. I liked it and had absolutely no idea (like most songs those days with references to drugs and sex) what the heck they were talking about. Like Betty Wright's cassette I played over and over, twenty years after its 70's release. Those songs would eventually take on new meaning as my life went on. My all-time favorite artist is Helen Folasade Adu, also known as Sade. Thanks to my older sister, Alma, who had all of her cassettes growing up, I became a lifelong fan. I was finally able to see her in concert in June 2011 thanks to my other sister Liz! Speaking of my sister Liz, there was a whole lot of Prince in rotation. She absolutely loved him!

The Jackson's, of course, and always playing some-where in the background of all that was the country music my dad listened to. Kenny Rogers, Randy Travis, Willy Nelson and Garth Brooks. I was planning to take him to see Garth live in Central Park before he died. Quite the diverse collection of artists in my life's soundtrack, I'm proud of that. I listened to all of the boy groups like The Boys, New Edition, Troop, Jodeci, Silk and H-Town (pretty sure I'm forgetting some).

My friends and I always picked a favorite out of each group. My bedroom walls were covered with clippings of various artists whose videos I would watch after school on Video Music Box (Channel U and 31). I took trips with my dad to the local convenience store so he could play the lottery, and I could make a b-line to the magazine rack to get the latest WordUp and RightOn. My whole closet door was dedicated to

James Todd Smith because I was his number one fan! If you know, you know, the ladies love Cool James.

Amongst my favorite Tapes/CD's of all time, meaning I played them endlessly once I got my hands on them, was anything Sade, Alanis Morissette - Jagged Little Pill, Mary J Blige - My Life, Lauren Hill - The Miseducation of Lauren Hill (dah), Deangelo - Brown Sugar, Bob Marley - Legend, Tracy Chapman - Tracy Chapmen, A Tribe Called Quest - Midnight Marauders, John P. Kee and the New Life Community Choir - We Walk by Faith and John Legend - Get Lifted. So many good memories in the music, thanks to the hundreds of CDs I ordered from Columbia House. Let's not forget the 98.7 Kiss FM DJ Red Alert mixtapes and 107.5 WBLS Quiet Storm slow jams that I'd stay up to record off my dual cassette stereo system. It was a good time to be alive, and I was definitely thankful for every moment I was. Oh, and Tupac's not dead (don't fight me on it).

My bucket list was never far from my mind. I accepted Christ as my personal savior and was baptized in my family church at twelve. Now I had secured my place in heaven for whenever it was I died. I should pause and mention I have unofficial ADHD, meaning I'm absolutely sure I have it, but I have not been clinically diagnosed. Absolutely certain of it, you'll most likely conclude the same, but stick with me.

Growing up a 90's kid, I was very aware of my

mortality. This made me a master planner, perfectionist and ultimate control freak, complete with OCD tendencies. I know, scary, right?! There was a place for everything, and everything was in its place. If you went into my room when I wasn't home and touched something, I was going to know about it. When death has let you know there are some things you can't control, you try very hard to control what you can. I developed anxiety and stomach ulcers by the age of 16 because when you are a teenager trying to get through high school to check graduation off your bucket list and hoping you make it to happily ever after before you die, it can be a little stressful. Looking back now, therapy would have been a great idea, but it wasn't a thing black families did back then. At least none I knew of. In God, we trust, and you couldn't do both God and therapy. The tears I've cried already writing this book have let me know there are some feelings I still need to process. Not only is therapy a great idea, but it's not too late to go.

I made lifelong friends growing up. I wasn't athletic or in any school clubs like most of them, but we had other things in common, like boys! I had major crushes that would last from elementary school till high school, and I was probably the only 13 year old during that time who had the same boyfriend for over a year. Why? Well, we were going to get married, of course! Shout out to my first teenage love. He cheated on me, and we broke up, but I'd gotten to experience it, and for me, that was at least something I could say I'd lived to do. I met my bestie in the 4th grade, and she's still my bestie today. She's the first person I knew with three-way calling. Although I had lucked up and got my sister's personal line when she went off to college, it was the three-way that would come in handy when I had her break up with any boy I'd figure out wasn't marriage material. "Jamie doesn't want to date you anymore." She's a straight shooter, whereas I was always worried about hurting feelings. I definitely started people-pleasing early.

High School days were bitter-sweet. Some of the best and worst years of my teenage life. Shout out to F.H.S Warriors Blue and Gold. I can remember hearing the marching band playing at the football games from my house. I remember homecoming dances and going to eat at Somerset Diner afterward. Going to the Kendall Park Roller Skating Rink on Sundays. Reciting whole episodes of Martin in history class and screaming for the boys in the High School talent shows.

Almost twenty-one! I could die soon, you know? I remember getting really depressed my senior year at the thought of moving on beyond graduation. The digital era wasn't what it is today with Facebook and FaceTime and ways to stay connected. These people were all I knew since my babysitting days and K-12. I would potentially never see them again. A lot to think about. It weighed heavily on me. I just wanted to go to sleep and wake up at 23, having done all I planned to do in-between. I planned to become a neonatal nurse through 2 years in community college and 3 years at The University of Delaware. A career inspired by my oldest niece being born prematurely at just one pound and miraculously defying all odds that she would live back in 1979. A 5-year plan since I'd taken my SATs twice and gotten the same disappointing score. It was a change from just graduating high school and would add a couple of years onto completing my bucket list. Now I had to live to be at least 23.

1. Graduate High School.
2. Graduate College
3. Get married.
4. Buy a house.

While planning out my education, I'd also been planning out my marriage. One Sunday in church a couple of years earlier, I'd seen this young couple with their twins. The husband was so attentive to the children, always getting up and taking them out when needed. Just like my dad was with us. Imagine my surprise when he turned up in youth bible study, and I found out he was my age! Full beard and goatee, but only 15 and SINGLE. My friend said she knew him and would set us up. He called, not right away, but he did call one night when I was home, watching Whitney Houston and

Kevin Costner in The Bodyguard. We talked for hours filling each other in on the past fifteen years. His parents were still together, in the church, he was close to his sisters (not his wife and kids, lol), and so after about a month, we were dating 1/1/93. He was the one!

We had your typical High School on again, off again break-ups over the next five years. I would get raped in-between one of those times, further solidifying there was no one else for me. I used to say date-raped because I knew who the person was, which made me feel like it wasn't as bad. A strange way of trying to fix it for myself. I told my sister Pearl about it when it happened because I told her everything. I was so stupid to put myself in that situation, and although I said, "NO" several times with my face pressed into the floor, hot tears running into the dingy basement carpet, I should have run, I should have yelled! I blamed myself.

Was I still a virgin? Oh My God! Did that count?! My sister assured me I was fine, it would be ok, and no, that didn't count. She also made it clear I could most certainly NEVER tell my dad. She said to keep it to myself, that some things were better left unsaid, and my dad would not be able to handle it. I believed her. She was always right. I know that man would have lost his life a lot sooner than he did breaking up a bar fight some years later if my dad had found out what he had done to his baby girl. I took the blame and moved on.

It would bring no good to anyone repeating it. Although, I would repeat a few times more in years to come to let others know "me too." If that man represented the kind of men I had to look forward to meeting then NO THANK YOU!

My teenage relationship was something I needed to make work. The break-up was off, and no matter what other interest came up, he was the one. I skipped the prom because who needs that when you're planning for a wedding. Graduated High School Class of '95. Started college, but didn't turn out to be "college material." After failing all but African American studies my first semester, I decided to stick to the initial bucket list. My Bestie was working with her parents at a corporate Fortune 500 company at the time, and her dad helped me get hired. Two years later, I married my high school sweetheart at 21. I purchased my first house at 22.

Turns out it was my childhood home my mom didn't want to maintain after my dad died and had put up for sale. CHECK, CHECK and CHECK! I lived long enough to experience all I ever wanted and was on my way to my happily ever after! At least that's what it looked like from the outside, or maybe just through my rose-colored glasses. You see, the perfectionist in me would try very hard over the next ten years to make it so. Have you ever wanted something so bad you're willing to look past every sign, red flag, gut check or literal audible voice that says it's something else? You are determined to see what you want to see?!

Call me crazy, you won't be the first! You pair perfectionism with the control freak, and you get a hot mess that looks like she has it all together. That was me. It just wasn't something I could see from the inside looking out, yet. After all, I was the one who had the career, husband, house and yes, eventually the kids. Doesn't get any more perfect than every box checked off and everything I said you wanted since the age of nine. The thing is, at 9 years old or even 21, for that matter, you don't really know who you are. Let alone what you want, only what you think you do. That's my story, at least. The human brain doesn't stop developing till the age of 25, but you couldn't convince me of that then. I had a plan, and I was now on borrowed time!

As far as I knew, the man I married, who I will refer to as "Ex," was jokingly and then not so jokingly the closest any of my dad's girls had gotten to marrying someone like him. He was easy-going, no fuss, and along for the plan I mapped out for us. I was sure of myself and confident in my ability to execute this plan for happily ever after. I did whatever was needed to ensure success. If it looked like eating peanut butter and jelly or tuna fish sandwiches every day at work to help save for my first apartment, so be it. Make a plan, stick to the plan and if it doesn't work, make another plan and stick to that one and if that one doesn't work....you get the picture.

It's a futile attempt to orchestrate perfection. I see it now, too, because hindsight is 20/20, but at the time, it made perfect sense.

I did NOT want to have children when we got married. I figured I had my nieces and nephews (11 by then) and couldn't wrap my head around why anyone would want to bring children into this crazy, scary world. Speaking of a crazy, scary world, I wanted to travel it! That plan would change when Ex said he wanted to start a family one year into our marriage. This shouldn't have come as a surprise given our premarital counseling with our pastor, but I failed to make the connection at the time. You see, my pastor had us take one of those personality tests. The only red flag that came back was in the area of what we each needed and what we were willing to give. I needed an 8, and I was willing to give an 8. Ex needed an 8 but was only willing to give a 3. Our pastor explained this combination could cause concern in that I needed more than he was willing to give. This may play out in me wanting children and devoting all my time to them to feel needed or open the door for an extramarital affair to fill that gap. I had no concerns with either, I didn't plan to have any children, and I would NEVER have an affair! When Ex proposed we start a family, I explained I needed some time.

Time to plan, of course! I then came up with a new plan which would give me five years and no only child (two no more than three). Five years turned into four when 9-11 happened, a trigger that reminded me I had a new item on my bucket list to complete before I died, and tomorrow wasn't promised. If I was going to experience motherhood, I better get a move on. I scheduled a doctor's visit, stopped taking the pill and started taking prenatal vitamins. I tracked my cycle, which was regular and always on time, thanks to the pill. I printed my ovulation calculator and stuck it on the fridge. I set up the baby's room over the years, purchased furniture to match the crib my sister had passed down to me and started picking up little "OH, this will be cute!" stuff here and there. Everything was in my old bedroom, covered in plastic, awaiting the pregnancy. When the time came, I got pregnant on our first try!

Everything was going according to the plan. Well, Until Ex moved out of our bedroom shortly after my pregnancy announcement. He said I was acting differently, being mean and blamed the pregnancy. He withdrew to the guest room downstairs in our bi-level home. Whoa, I didn't see that coming! Definitely NOT part of the plan, and I wasn't ready. The pregnancy was new to us both, and I figured whatever adjustments we had to make, we would make them together, in the same bedroom. My feelings were crushed, and I worried about what the next eight months would be like. What would happen when I got fat?! Would he leave the house completely? It would be six years later that Ex would confess the true reason for him moving downstairs was nothing to do with my pregnancy. Once again, I'd be caught off guard, hurt, anxious and agitated. Another monkey wrench in my plan for happily ever after. Why was this proving to be so freakin' hard?!

It didn't add up. This was so unlike the man I thought I married. In hindsight, this should have caused a waving red flag. I thought Ex would be thrilled. After all, it was his idea to add children into the marriage equation. In years to come, Ex would share more insight on this time in my life as well. Turns out, unlike me, Ex had made a connection to what my pastor had said during premarital counseling and the reason that he suggested we start a family was to "occupy my time." Ex didn't really want an 8 like the test had shown. He very much liked his alone time.

The fact that Ex left me pregnant with our baby when we should have celebrated the expectancy honestly confused me. The pregnancy had changed him. Or was it me, and I just couldn't tell because I was on the inside of it? I heard terms like pregnancy brain, and my body was changing due to the pregnancy hormones. Maybe it really was me! I had to figure this out. The last thing I wanted was to have family and friends who were all so happy about us having a baby, burdened with our marriage drama. This was supposed to be a happy time, and I remembered some things are better left unsaid. I know now that communication is essential to any resolution and that you should absolutely use your voice to advocate for your needs and express your concerns. Good ole hindsight! At the time, what I knew was my plan was NOT working out. I had missed something. I had to find out what, so I could fix it. I mentioned my situation to a male co-worker, asked was this normal behavior for a man? He said it was not.

This new dynamic was strange, but I had to make it work. I was upstairs pregnant, watching TV and Ex was downstairs playing his video game or watching basketball (I assumed). I kept myself busy, took tae-kwon-do, and enrolled in a vocational school for cosmetology because part of my planning was deciding if I wanted to go back to corporate after I had my children. I had my full time during the day and school at night during the week. I had my sisters and my small circle of close friends. This could work. It had to work for my happily ever after.

This action plan of staying busy and going through the motions would help mask what I was really feeling: loneliness, insignificant and unlovable. I was almost sure I'd made a mistake in believing I married someone that would never make me feel this way. The perfectionist in me doesn't sit well with mistakes, especially ones I can't fix. So convincing myself that it had to be me actually helped. If it was Ex, there would be too many unknown variables. Too many things I couldn't plan out, and that would mean who knows what for my happily ever after. But if it was me, I could fix it! I could do better. I could change. If the pregnancy had changed me so much that Ex didn't even want to be in the same room with me, then it was a matter of time before that changed back, right?! This gave Ex his space, and he'd eventually miss sleeping in the bed next to me, right?! Eventually, Ex did come back upstairs to our bedroom. Three months later, but by then, it was already too late.

Reflection

What childhood fears or insecurities have
you let limit you? How will you overcome
them?

When I was younger I was scared that _____

_____

_____

_____

_____

_____

_____

_____

_____

_____

_____

2

KILLING ME SOFTLY

I slept with that male co-worker I was getting advice from. I was two months pregnant with my daughter. "I am not my worst mistake." It took me years to believe that. Yup, while Ex was downstairs escaping my pregnancy hormones, so he said, I was upstairs chit-chatting on the phone with this new "friend" from work about how inattentive, selfish and neglectful I thought Ex was. I wasn't expressing how hurt I was and that I felt lonely and unloved, yet apparently, that had come through loud and clear. I was leading with, "Do you believe this guy? Crazy, right!" This was safe enough, wasn't it? We were simply talking on the phone and watching the Soul Food series together on TV. "Tell him I said what's up!"

Ex would say on his way downstairs. Ex was relieved I had someone to occupy my time and entertain my conversations, besides him. Another red flag I would miss.

You may recall the conversation we had with our pastor. I needed an 8. I wanted attention, and I wanted to feel wanted. It was nice to have someone to talk to about what was going on and not burden my family. They wouldn't be happy, and if they weren't happy, then I wasn't happy. That's a lie I believed for a long time. The planner in me didn't plan for catching feelings and the cliche "one thing lead to another" one evening after meeting up with co-workers after work to hang out. Why? Because remember, I would NEVER have an affair! "I don't know how people can be so dumb." I had said that. **Lifestyle Success Tip: Pride comes before the fall!**

So now the person I would never be, I was! Trust me when I tell you talking to male co-workers or friends about your marital problems is a very bad idea. If you ever wondered what giving the devil a foothold looks like, that's it! Now, I'm not claiming the devil made me do it, but trust and believe he was close by with his popcorn. I sunk into a depression, but no one would question me laying in bed all day or crying all the time. It was assumed to be those dang pregnancy hormones! No one would ask what happened?

So I wouldn't have to lie, and I wouldn't have to tell.

I would love to blame those pregnancy hormones, but I have to own my mess. It was me, but not who I thought I was or wanted to be. I tried to make it almost as if it never happened. I didn't just do that did I? Let's move on and never speak of it again. That worked until it was spoken of again by that male co-worker, and all contact ended. Of course, I repented, and God in all His loving grace forgave me, but I would carry the guilt and shame for a very long time afterward. One key to forgiveness is when you're on the receiving end, you have to accept and receive it. Otherwise, the guilt and shame will continue to show up whenever it wants to, without invitation and wear out its welcome. Five years later, I finally confessed the affair during one of our many marriage counseling sessions.

This was also when I realized I'd been holding my breath that whole time. During everything that happened in between those five years, I let the guilt and shame justify it. Red flag, after red flag, after red flag. I'd feel that I had brought on myself by keeping this dirty secret in the back of my mind. A secret that was killing me softly.

It is important to understand that everyone is responsible for their own actions. I remember the counselor turning to Ex and asking him what he was doing during this time. "Where were you?" he asked. "Downstairs." You see, it is easy to point the finger at other people, but you have to own your own stuff and what part, if any, you may have played.

Looking for the lessons during things can be hard, but the sooner you learn the lesson, the better. Lessons are meant to better you, to grow you. Sure, there are some I wish I could have done without, but I wouldn't be who I am now if not for them. I am not my worst mistake. It is something I have done, not who I am. I say that to remind you of the same. You are not your worst mistake, and it does not have to define you. We serve a forgiving God, hand the guilt and shame over. Know that you get to choose to show up differently. **Lifestyle Success Tip: Own your sh*t!**

I had to come back from my guilt trip and pull myself together. I had a baby to think about, and so I needed yet another plan. I know, I know! During this time, it was still who I was. I hadn't quite figured out even though I had to be on something like Plan E by now that you can't plan everything. Are you still with me? Good! So, I needed to get Ex back upstairs. I was not going to tell him about the affair. I wasn't ready for the worst-case scenario. I justified this by telling myself that God had forgiven me and no good would come from telling him. I would take it to my grave. Some things are better left unsaid. **Lifestyle Success Tip: Get it out and over with!**

Dirty little secrets will try to take you out. It is not

worth the internal torment. Absolutely consider the feelings of others and be tactful about how you share them. Maybe even choose a safe place which may be with a counselor or therapist. Whatever works best for you, but own your mistakes and be ready to accept the consequences. So NOW, back to my plan to get Ex back upstairs.

Plan - "Upstairs" went down while out at dinner for a cousin's birthday. We were still out in the streets like everything was everything, meanwhile, home life was a whole wreck. Going through the motions and putting on smiles, because you don't go airing out dirty laundry. Something I would unintentionally get really good at over time. Had you asked me, I would have told you we were fine. So anyway, that night, I simply leaned over and said with a straight face, "You need to come back upstairs." and that was that.

EYES WIDE SHUT

What I refer to as eyes wide shut is being fully aware of a situation but acting like it doesn't exist. Moving about like you don't see that mess you're walking around in. I also call it denial! For me, happily ever after was still in sight. Mind you, nothing about any of what I was experiencing indicated it was anything close to that actually existing. If anything, it was the direct opposite. What would it mean for me, though, if I had to accept that? Was I just going to die, never having experienced it? Never knowing what that love was like? I could still make this work! I just had to do better, be better! Even as I write this now, I want to go back and shake myself. But this is my story, the good, the bad and I wish it never happened. One thing I can appreciate now is that it gets better. Just not yet.

So Ex and I are back in the same bedroom. That's about it, but good enough. Once I have the baby and these hormones leave my body, things will get better. In the meantime, I'm working and saving to stay home from work for a year to be with my daughter. I wanted to make sure Ex would be a present parent, so I was sure not to burden him with extra financial need and having to work any more than he already did. I was executing this plan in full mommy mode now. The thought of having to leave my baby and go back to 40 hour work weeks was disheartening. My sister Pearl and a partner of hers owned two daycare facilities and I had watched her stay home and raise my nieces and nephews, so I knew this was an option for me.

The only difference was her husband made enough to support this, Ex did not. Since I made a considerable amount more, I had to be the one to make it happen, and I did. Every month while out on FMLA on what would be my usual payday, I would transfer my net payment into my checking from my savings and continue as normal. Making sure I paid offering, grocery shopped, paid the bills, etc. My daughter was born in July 2002. I purchased my husband his dream car by that October. The perfect new dad gift/I still feel guilty about the affair gift. We had fallen into a new normal, and life was good again. If this were a movie, the music would change right about now to indicate something is about to go down.

Let me set the scene. I've been home from work now for four months. Baby girl and I are living our best life. Ex is acting normal, and all is well at home. I'm nursing my daughter, which I did a full year (1. Because I wanted to and 2. Because she refused to take a bottle.) and the house phone rings, remember those? So yea, I answer in the kitchen, and the woman on the other end is calling from a MasterCard company. She asks for Ex by name. "Yes, ma'am, but no ma'am. I mean, that's my husband, but he's not home. He doesn't have a MasterCard anyway. There must be some type of mistake." It had to be because I handled all the bills and money because coming to the marriage, Ex had run up credit card debt in college, which we had to pay off, so I knew he was no good at managing money. A red flag I didn't know then would turn out to be so important. Come to think of it, Ex had mentioned something about someone trying to steal his identity a few weeks ago. This must be what Ex was speaking about. "Can you see what type of charges are on the card, ma'am? I think someone has stolen my husband's identity." She let me know she wasn't authorized to speak with me and would try calling back or his cell phone. I went on to explain I needed to clear this issue up, that I handled all the bills, and we had no debt. I was at home with a newborn baby at the moment and would appreciate it if this could be settled, so she didn't have to call back. Wait, she said cell phone? "What cell phone number do you have? That may go to the culprit that stole my husband's identity?" She read me the number, and my stomach churned. "That's my husband's cell."

There was a long silence between the two of us, and then she spoke. This time, she was closer to the phone. She was no longer doing her job. She was about to help a sista out. She let me know the P.O. box the statements were being sent to, and read notes from cash advances, where Ex had claimed hardship from me being out of work and him having to buy baby furniture, none of which he had paid for! She read charges back through the years, Xbox's and NBA game tickets Ex had told me he won from raffles at work. DAMMIT! We conceived my daughter that weekend we went to that NBA game! As far back as including the diamond upgrade to my engagement ring. Ex had explained the secret savings account that showed up in the paperwork buying our house in 1999 was for that. Guess not. This wasn't a red flag. This was a red flashing neon jumbo screen-sized sign that read "OVER." Whoever you are, Sis, good lookin out!

Who the hell was this person I had married?! Abort all plans! THIS was not going to end in happily ever after. I called my sister and filled her in on the whole conversation. Then I called him at work to say I knew and questioned where all this money had gone? It most definitely had NOT gone to the care of our home or daughter. A grand total of over $26,000+ worth of debt! I felt duped, so stupid for believing all those lies. I had damn near driven myself insane guilt-tripping over my secret, and here this man was living a double life! He was NOT who he said he was. A shock to everyone because he played his part so well. There has to be a reason. Why would Ex do this? All the time's Ex said he was going to pay money towards the ring, where had he gone? You know what? It really didn't matter. I was not staying to figure it out. My sister came right over, and we rummaged through drawers and dug through closets. That amount of money has to be there somewhere. It wasn't. Nowhere that we could find it anyway. I still never got a believable answer to where, what or who all the money had been spent on.

I went to my pastor for an annulment. He advised me it didn't work like that. I have to laugh at that now, but I was still so young at the time that it made sense to me that false pretenses or something had to get me out of this. This was so unfair! Ex was a complete fraud! The whole marriage had been a lie! When I tell you I was upset, I was UPSET!!! Not hurt because I didn't know this person I was dealing with now. I was PISSED OFF! I wanted a divorce and to get rid of this imposter that messed up my happily ever after. The biggest upset of all, I was going to be a single parent! I didn't even want to have kids but agreed because Ex said he wanted them. **Lifestyle Success Tip: Never have children for someone else.**

Resentment built. "I just hope I get to see her." that's what Ex said. "SEE HER?! You're lucky I don't pack her up with you! Oh, and by the way, you owe me another kid, put it in a cup or whatever, but we agreed on no only children, and I don't want two baby daddies." That was me. Even in my upset and world crashing down around me, I was working out a plan! There was no way, of course, I would have let him take my daughter. That was what had built the resentment. I had been fine with my decision to never know motherhood, but now Ex and his big ideas had introduced me to love like never before. I had gotten to grow this amazing little human inside of me, and she changed my life forever. I could not just rid myself of Ex and go back to who I was. I was a mom now. Thanks to this stranger in my house, I would have to do motherhood alone. We ended up in marriage counseling which was pretty much me trying to get my pastor to say it was ok for us to get a divorce, and Ex trying to look like he was confused as to why we were there and play the victim.

We are both the babies in our family, and so when my initial upset at finding out about the debt and this imposter lead me to my pastor's office for a divorce, it would be his parents and my sister Pearl who would convince us to stay together for the baby and for the love we'd both said we still had for each other. The love? Had either of us known what love was? If we had, we would have known what we had was not it. Pretending it was would not help matters. We had convenience and time, two things I don't ever suggest being the reason you stay somewhere you know you shouldn't be.

The love revelation wouldn't come to me then. At that time, all I needed was a new plan. One part of my earlier plan that had not changed was I didn't want my daughter to be an only child. I have such a close bond with my siblings, and I wanted that for my children. The plan for baby number two was still on. Due to the fact that we weren't "connecting" often, I know the exact day I got pregnant. "You want another baby, right?" January 13, 2004, I conceived my son. He was born September 2004, and by that following March, I would find out there was more money and more debt after refinancing our house to pay off the initial $26K, Ex's new car and Ex's student loan. I found the statement stuck to the inside of the recycling bin. He didn't know what I was talking about, he said. But I had proof! I should have seen the loan payments to the credit union coming out of his paycheck, but he'd been doctoring his paystubs month after month so that it didn't show up. Duped once again! Shame on me. *Lifestyle Success Tip: Don't ever give someone a chance to play you twice*

Reflection

Do you have any secrets that are killing you
softly? It's time to release yourself Sis.

I am not my worst mistake. _____

_____

_____

_____

_____

_____

_____

_____

_____

_____

_____

3

I CAN FIX IT

One last try, because this was exhausting! Every lie I fell for, I would lose a little more confidence in myself and the plan. I mean, seriously, if boo boo the fool was a person, Ex surely thought I was her. I felt like such an idiot and dumber and dumber each time I found out something else. Another lie that would trace back to a string of lies to cover each other that I had believed along the way. Ex definitely didn't love me, respect me or appreciate me. It was like it was one big game he was playing with my life and now our kid's lives too. Eventually, I'd accept that Ex was just a liar, and I really did not like this guy! BUT if I can win in the end, does it really matter how the game was played? Another plan is in full effect. My happily ever after was back in play even if it was with this person I felt like I had been misled into marrying. I figured if we are going to stay together and make it through financial issues, material affairs, lies and despair, then surely it was for a reason. I wasn't sure exactly what that reason was, but there had to be one, right?! I was able to excel in every other area of my life, so I knew I had it in me. My kids had skin in the game now. I thought, "I can fix this!"

After the year out with my daughter, I returned to work but planned out retirement from corporate after my son. I took a volunteer package and became a stay-at-home mom with the payout. I started working part-time with my sister at her daycare, and life was good again for a little while. I loved the freedom away from the corporate world, and when you saw me, you saw my kids. I knew life like this wouldn't last if I couldn't supplement my income. I made a plan for us to move. I had attempted this two years prior but had chickened out when they started talking about layoffs on my job. Now my fate would no longer be left for a corporation to decide. I would find a way to control my own income and give my family the fresh start we needed! Two of my sisters and I hopped in the car with my daughter and took a ride to Pennsylvania. After going a little too far in and realizing the properties I had initially scheduled to see were not in any area we'd be welcomed in, we headed back to New Jersey, where insurance and taxes were high, but where we were welcomed. Right before heading back across the border, we noticed a sign for new homes.

We decided it wouldn't hurt to take a look. We had come all this way after all. Up the mountain, we saw these beautiful new homes being built on this golf course and there, walking down the street, was a black man pushing his daughter in a stroller. Ok! So we're welcome here! We rolled up next to him and rolled down our window to inquire. He pointed out which home was his and told us he'd be right back. He returned with a Realtor hat on and business cards. He would sell all three of us new construction homes and become our family Realtor and friend. I knew then my home would be there on top of the hill on that golf course. I would build a house just like his, but better!

We were moving to Pennsylvania! New state, new home and new beginnings. This was just what we needed. This would fix it! I had a plan for everything, sticky notes and notebooks full of ideas, plans and numbers...oh, the numbers. I can make a dollar out of fifteen cents. I had done some work with investors and looked into real estate. Now was the perfect time. I invested in a property that I rented out and built a 5 bedroom 5500 square feet house on that golf course. My sister Pearl built her house right across the street and my sister Alma built hers less than 20 minutes away. Pearl and I took a two-week accelerated course to get our Real Estate Licenses and joined our Realtor's team. We were all set! Ex and I found an amazing church and rededicated our lives back to Christ. We joined Bible studies and got engaged in the community. The new construction market was booming with buyers, Pearl and I partnered up as buyers' agents, and I was making more than I'd made in corporate. Yea, life was good again. Then it wasn't.

A year later, an altar call at church one Sunday morning would result in us back in marriage counseling. Maybe it's a red blanket by now, or fancy quilt work of all the red flags (sigh). Who the heck knows?! What I do know is I felt like I was now officially THAT woman. The one people whisper about for being so dumb for putting up with his crap and so stupid for staying. I kept thinking of all the time I'd invested, and all the time wasted if I left.

It was here that the 5-year confession I mentioned came out. I found out what Ex always being downstairs was all about. Our counselor suggested we each come clean with everything so we could start again and move on towards healing our relationship. Aha! That's why I haven't been able to fix this. My dirty little secret has been blocking my blessings. It was blocking my happily ever after. We needed a clean slate! I had been trying to start fresh with that filth lingering in the air. I knew what I had to do.

I confessed my affair. Then wouldn't you know it, even though we had supposedly already had everything out in the open, I found out that Ex had made a friend of his own and he and his co-worker had been going out together instead of "working late." He was initially upset about the affair and pointed out although he'd been going out with this woman, he'd never slept with her. Ex noted some years later that it was not because he didn't want to or try to sleep with the women he talked to over the years, but that something would always come up to interrupt him. I guess that was his way of making himself look good, and me feel bad. It did neither. I get it, because I can see now exactly who Ex is. I hid my secret affair for years, and the upset over it didn't even last two sessions. Ex said he had done so much over the years it didn't seem fair to hold it against me. Ex loved looking like the good guy.

Now with everything out in the open, I guess we could try again. I just had to get over one hard truth that came out. Not the other woman. I wasn't into Ex like that anymore. It was why he had married me in the first place when clearly happily ever after wasn't on his radar. "Because I knew you'd make a good wife, and if I didn't marry you, someone else would." My sister tried to convince me Ex didn't mean it like that, but I knew he did. I learned then, don't ask questions you don't want the answer to. Our counselor gave us a plan to help cultivate some healthy habits and set out to try this marriage thing one more time. Staying true to what this toxic cycle in our relationship had already shown me, it would appear like everything was good for a little while until receipts would show up and I would find out nothing had changed. Ex was still the same. I was beyond exhausted at this point. I was having IBS episodes on a regular basis, my sleep pattern was non-existent. I was running on fumes and too busy being drained to take notice. Like many women I know, I just kept going. I still had to show up and be mom, sister, friend, etc. Caught up in being there for everyone else, I didn't take the time to pause and think about who I was or wasn't being for myself.

As if I wasn't dealing with enough, my attention got diverted when we found ourselves in the middle of the 2006 - 2008 Real Estate Market crash. Talk about your series of unfortunate events. I had a tenant in my investment property with a lease to buy contract who would leave me high and dry by filing bankruptcy and walking away from the deal. With no one building or buying houses, commissions dwindled. I struggled trying to pay two mortgages in an effort not to mess up my 700+ credit score, only to lose both houses and a third property when I was forced to file bankruptcy myself, at the end of 2008. That January of 2008, I'd started reaching out to my old corporate contacts to see if I could get back in and applied to other companies online. Three months, then six months went by when my first interview at a telecom company in PA came through. The job was offered at an hourly rate that was a fourth of what I'd been making four years prior when I left my corporate Project Manager position. I turned it down. That wouldn't even cover the pre-k program I wanted my son to start.

The officers kept showing up with their stickers and flyers for the sheriff's sales, and bill collectors kept calling. Never in my life had I been late in paying a bill. This was so humiliating! Not only was my happily ever after not happening, but I had lost my job, the investment properties and soon my home. I had close friends help me out with clothes for the kids and monetary donations. I am truly grateful for my tribe that was there for me. I was helping pick up and watch some of my friend's kids while being home. I eventually had to let them know I could not afford to do the favor because I couldn't afford the gas money to get to and from. I started referring to this as my 'Job' experience. I was so emotionally and mentally drained that I didn't have a plan of my own for the first time. I had no clue how to fix it. I took it to God and left it with Him. I was reminded of Job in the bible and thought if God had thought enough of me to say, "Have you considered my servant Jamie" I would not let Him down. I believed He would see me through, just like He had Job.

Lifestyle Success Tip: God's plan is always better than yours!

I can remember my mom calling from New Jersey to check up on me. She said she had not been able to sleep thinking about what my family was going through. She asked if I had been sleeping and if I had found a job yet. I told her I had slept better than I had in a long time.

I didn't know how, but I knew God would work it out. Fast forward to November 2008, I still hadn't found a job, the bankruptcy was final, and now Ex's job had informed him they were transferring his role to a call center in North Carolina. Moving there wasn't an option for us, so he'd have to find another position. We had one month before the sheriff would lock us out of our home. I prayed and continued to trust God. It was all I knew to do. I know it sounds like it's just the thing to say, but really, I had exhausted all alternatives. I wish I could say God was my first source, but I am sure if I hadn't been too worn out to function and think straight, I would have come up with another plan.

The lowest I can recall my bank account getting was around $35. I was making grilled cheese for our dinners. My sister was helping me look for a new place. Still no job, but hoping every day that the call would come from my old corporate job. Ex made just enough for us to get by, but not enough to cover rent or mortgage. I paid the tithes, kept the utilities on, and we never went hungry. All glory to God! When you hear folks say He may not come when you want Him, but He is always on time...I am a witness this is true. Ex heard back on a new position on a Monday, so he'd stay employed. I received a call to interview back at my corporate job that Wednesday. I got the job!!!

One of my big concerns with moving was my daughter having to switch schools. That Friday, my sister found a townhouse for rent a block over from our home. If this place worked out, my daughter wouldn't even have to change bus stops! But with my bankruptcy and no steady check yet, who would rent to me? I went to see the place and loved it! The realtor that showed me the property suggested I write a letter to the owner explaining my situation and include my credit report I had a copy of from the bankruptcy so he could see the sharp dip that matched my story. The market crash was a big topic in the news by now, the owner was understanding. Without hesitation, we were approved to move in within the month. That would give me time to start working and provide security as well as move out of our home before they put us out. My God is faithful!!! I learned that I couldn't fix it, and even when I think I have control, I don't. I learned to put my trust in God!

At this point, Ex and I were both on autopilot and

going through the motions. I was back to being a working mom, which meant commuting an hour back down to New Jersey for work, and my sister watching my kids. I'd made our new house a home for my children and moved about my days in mom mode. If I ever got the idea that there was a chance at happily ever after, I was now reluctant to try. Each try had gotten fewer and farther between. Even with that being the case, no one worked harder to make a marriage work than I did on mine! I did what the books said, and I listened to women at church. I willed all the power of a praying wife to help me like this person that felt like a stranger. This was what people meant, I guess, when they say thick or thin. I guess this is the real work people talk about with marriage. Only, I could almost swear the nicer I was, the meaner Ex was. The sex was seldom, and I can remember it being too hot to touch or my foot crossing the invisible line in our bed and his leg slowly moving away. I remember the spot on the wall I would focus on. I could NOT fix this. I wasn't good enough, and apparently, I was just too hard for him to love.

Slowly but surely, any feelings I had left or tried to cultivate faded. My prayer shifted from God, "Give me a passion for my husband." to God, "Help me not to care." You see, it wasn't that I was so in love with Ex. I had gotten over that back in 2002. I was still in love with the idea I wanted and believed that if I worked hard enough, I could have.

66

Happily ever after. There was just something in me despite all the red flags and signs. I could not let go of the idea that since I believed such a thing existed, I wanted to experience it. The fact that Ex refused to comply was just a great annoyance. I would point out couples, look at them, look at how they're friends, how come we can't be like that? Look at how he treats her. How come you can't treat me like that? *Lifestyle Success Tip: Don't compare your relationship to others, and definitely don't compare your significant other to anyone else.*

I can see in hindsight how difficult I made it to simply BE. My perfectionism made people around me feel like they had to be perfect. While I don't take responsibility for the lies, manipulation and emotional strain Ex caused me, I do own that I was not willing to fail. I was not willing to just let things be as they were. For someone that just wanted to be left alone, I made it very hard. I couldn't understand why I wasn't enough and why God didn't feel like I deserved this love. Had my affair sealed my fate. Maybe this was my punishment, and I would never know such a love. I walked around smiling on the outside and sad on the inside for a long time. Our marriage had been a smokescreen for many years at that point, feelings lost and walls built. It was a lunchtime conversation in March of 2010 that would lead to the very end. Ex asked me why I couldn't accept things for what they were. He stated he was a bad person, that does bad things. He didn't know what was wrong with him. He didn't know why I stayed married to him, but he couldn't be the husband I wanted him to be.

At the end of that call, we would both agree I would leave "us" alone and stop trying to make "us" something we would never be. We agreed that we would no longer try to be husband and wife (at least not the type I was looking for). We would instead focus on being mom and dad to the kids. I repeated this conversation to Ex in later years. He doesn't remember it. I remember it clearly because it was the day I finally surrendered my happily ever after.

I had enough going on at the time, processing what was happening to my sister. The chemo, the cancer markers, was it working? I cried so hard that day. I was reminded once again that tomorrow isn't promised, and you just never know. I went into mourning the marriage I always wanted but would never have. I walked through all the pain, the hurt, the anger and the shame. I replayed every scenario when I thought it was working, and then the other shoe would drop, and I would find out it wasn't. I thought about all the red flags I ignored that were so clear now. I was so angry at all the time lost, all the effort I put in, everything I put up with for it to come to this. I prayed to God because this, much like any other death, was almost too much to bear. I questioned God about why he had made me like this. Why couldn't I just be happy with what

I had and settle for good enough? Why couldn't I just not care if he loved me or not? Isn't that what people did, settle. Why did my heart ache for happily ever after if I was never meant to know it? Why couldn't I just be happy going through the motions like couples I knew that stayed together for their kids? This was a hard pill to swallow, and my only sounding board had enough going on in her life that I didn't dare bother her. I'd have to figure this out alone. *Lifestyle Success Tip: If you feel like you're made for more, you are!*

I spent a lot of time reflecting. I had to be honest with who I had become. I felt like my voice didn't matter. No matter how many times I had expressed what I wanted and needed, my concerns, opinions and feelings were overlooked or went unaddressed. I felt like I wasn't attractive or sexy because Ex would rather watch women on a computer screen than physically be with me. I remember thinking if I was going to feel this lonely, I might as well be alone. Yet here I was, stuck.

It would be at yet another family function that August that I'd move past it all. Hotel party with the music blasting and dance floor open. I needed relief. I need to do something fun! I hit the dance floor alone. Ex soon joined me...not for me, not for us, but so people wouldn't question why I was out there by myself. At the end of the night, Ex made sure I hadn't gotten any ideas about what happened. He made sure it was clear, though we'd danced the night away together on the dance floor, nothing between us had changed. For the first time, it wasn't Ex I had the problem with. It was ME! Life was too short. Why was I allowing this? Why had I agreed to those stupid terms? Why had I been so desperate? I resolved then, no more time feeling sorry for my situation, my mourning was over and so were we!

Losing your identity is not something anyone plans to do. It happens subtly. Little by little, each time, you shrink yourself to fit in a room. If you've ever had an opinion but didn't speak up because you were too embarrassed to share. You affirmed that still small voice that says your voice doesn't matter. If you've ever pretended something didn't bother you, that was truly extremely troubling. You devalued your feelings. Each time we do these things, a little bit of true identity drifts away. One day you'll look up from the middle of what feels like an ocean, scared, with no shore in sight and realize you don't know who you are. That's how it was for me.

SWEET SURRENDER

January 2010, my sister Pearl was diagnosed with stage 4 Lung Cancer. The initial news rocked my family. It was followed by some good news though. They said that it was isolated, and they could remove 1/3 of her lung, do a couple of rounds of radiation and get it all out. My sister stayed in God's ear, I would ask her what He was telling her, so I'd know what way to move. Was this a fight, or sweet surrender? When she said she would fight, I met her at the throne in prayer. **Lifestyle Success Tip: Prayer is your best weapon.**

On the day of her surgery, I waited with my mom and other sisters and her husband in the waiting room. We were prepared for the hours and hours they'd said it would be before she came out to the recovery room. We'd be there waiting. When the surgeon came out a whole lot sooner than expected, we were confused. Wow, that was fast! Why didn't he look like he had good news? "Is everything ok?" We'd find out that once they broke my sister's rib to get to her lung, they'd seen what the scans didn't show: a whole lot more cancer! They closed her back up without even bothering to remove it. He said she had about 3 to 6 months to live. With some chemo, they would try to slow it down. This, as you can imagine, was devastating news. My sister was not only a hero to me, but now both of my kids, she had the answers, so who would I go to? While we were worried about her, she was worried about us. Her nurse had told her the news before we got to her (my sister Alma still wants to fight that nurse). "Are you ok?" she asked. That's who she was, always thinking about everyone else.

Y'all, this was crazy! My sister had stage 4 Lung

Cancer! Not because she was a smoker, but because ten years earlier, she'd had walking pneumonia that left her with scar tissue on her lung. The doctor told her to keep an eye on it, and she'd need to get that checked on a regular basis. She never did. **Lifestyle Success Tip: Don't put your health on the back burner. Make your appointments, go to your follow-ups!**

She said she wanted to live, and so that would be the miracle I believed God for. She would LIVE! I had to surrender the worry to God and rest in that belief. Quality over quantity is what she wanted. She got just that! She lived for 2 more years, not the 3 to 6 months they initially gave her. She lived her life enjoying her journey. Loving her kids, grandson, helping out young girls through the church and laughing till her end. **Lifestyle Success Tip: Live your life, enjoy your journey.**

I wish I hadn't spent so much time trying to change things I couldn't control. I wish I had embraced the hard lessons for the character they were creating in me. When she checked into the hospital, I prayed for her to come home and just like my prayer for my dad, it received a confirmation that she would not leave the hospital alive. By the time I returned to the hospital to ask her what God was saying, she had traded her fight for sweet surrender. She declined the oxygen mask and simply stated to my sister Alma that God was with her. I knew God had told her the same thing He told me. I did get to see her. I did get to say goodbye. She died four days later on Valentine's Day, 2012. Those 2 years, she had LIVED, and that was the miracle we believed for. I miss her, but I know her soul is well, pain-free and at peace.

Reflection

What areas in your life are you trying to fix that
you need to release to God?

Dear God, I release the following areas of my life to you. _____

_____

_____

_____

_____

_____

_____

_____

_____

_____

_____

_____

4

SELF-LOVE FIRST

❝ Ok, Jamie, if Ex is not going to love you, YOU are!"

The idea of self-love was a new concept to me, but I embarked on the journey. My sister's fight with cancer made me appreciate the time I had, and I would not spend it trying to make someone else love me. The first voice I heard was my earthly father replaying in my head how many times he'd said, "You can do bad by yourself." The second voice was my heavenly Father reminding me I was fearfully and wonderfully made. I didn't know what loving myself looked like, but I knew I had to start somewhere. I started with treating myself. It had been years since I shopped for myself. My sisters were in pure shock when they realized I was wearing my maternity pants with the stomach pouch rolled down. I mean, they were comfy, so why not?! I'd grown out my hair because Ex said one day that long hair was sexier. That was the first to go! I don't know if they still do it, but Old Navy used to have an item of the week. No matter what it was, every week I bought it in my size. This was external work, but it was a start. The internal work was where the real transformation would happen.

My first affirmation was "I am enough!" It took me a long time to accept this as the truth. I am enough, and I am not that hard to love. The more reflection and realization of how far I was from the me I'd once been saddened me. There was no way I could go back to the 21-year-old girl, I was a woman now. I just didn't like the woman I was. I didn't like this woman that had silenced her voice, tried so hard to please people and been so busy trying to make everyone else happy that she'd left herself empty, questioning her self-worth, her value, and her ability to be loved. **Lifestyle Success Tip: Fill your cup first and serve out of your abundant overflow.**

I thought about the compromising situations I'd put myself in. I played back scenarios where I had shrunk myself because being myself was perceived as too much. The times I laughed too loud, talked too much, was too emotional, etc., made to feel shameful for expressing my sexuality. All these times, I'd shift, try to adjust to better fit into a box designed for someone else. Suppressing feelings, and a little bit of who I was each time. I thought about how much of myself I had lost over the years and how much of myself I had not taken the time to get to know. That poor little girl that wanted happily ever after so much she would lose herself trying to get it.

I felt bad for the twenty-one-year-old that got married and hadn't even finished developing. The girl that grew into a woman who had no idea who she was or what she really wanted. I would love her, and I would thank her for trying so hard, for fighting. I thanked that nine-year-old little girl who'd just been trying to process her brother's death and had lived with the stress and anxiety of the uncertainty of life. I thanked every part of me that had gotten me to that point for every lesson that had prepared me for who I was about to become. I was certain I would never be any of them again! I would be a combination of all of those former selves and experience life in a new way.

Dear Me,

Thank you for trying so hard. I will make sure it's not in vain. Thank you for doing your best. Even when you knew better and didn't do it, thank you for recovering from your mistakes.

Thank you for surviving the rape. Thank you for carrying the stress and anxiety around the uncertainty of death and all the sleepless nights worrying about happily ever after. All the talks, the prayers, the sacrifices you made trying to be loved. Thank you for every time you thought it was better to stay quiet when really you should have used your voice. I forgive you the times you thought less of yourself and played small. Thank you for both crying and laughing.

Thank you for never giving up on love. Thank you for embracing motherhood and loving your children with such deep love. Thank you for always valuing family. Thank you for keeping in touch with your friends and for letting go of the ones that didn't serve you well.

Thank you for accepting your flaws. Thank you for every smile and helping hand. Thank you for trusting the Lord and remaining hopeful. Thank you for finally letting go. Thank you for making the most of what was given to you and thank you for loving me just as I am. I needed it all to get to where I am right now. Thank you! I promise you our best is yet to come. I will make you proud!

Love, Me

I permitted myself to reinvent myself and to embrace the unknown. I started by reminding myself of the parts of me I loved. Like my smile, my laugh and my ability to make others do the same. I thought about my kids and wondered what little moments I may have missed being so caught up with happily ever after. I thought about my future, and I knew I did not want my life (as it was), to be the rest of my life. I could not stay under what seemed to be a dark cloud that covered me when I walked into my house. I will suffocate, I will die here. That was my reality. I lost myself along the long journey, but I would love myself enough to reinvent myself, embrace all the things I love, and cultivate new things to replace those I didn't. I realized how much I relied on my sister's opinion once I didn't have it. Not wanting to burden her with my situation, I discovered I actually had an opinion of my own.

Though I have always been very opinionated, my opinion didn't always count for much. Being the baby, I was conditioned to believe I needed to be told what to do. I would buck up against that idea for sure, but I didn't trust that I knew what was best for me at the end of the day. In case you have not been able to tell by now, my sisters and I are extremely close. They had all been married first, had their kids first and obviously lived longer. Therefore it made sense to me that they knew more. Pearl was our family matriarch, oldest, wisest, and her opinion was to be respected. No matter if you agreed or not, you bowed down. Hearing my own thoughts without inviting others in allowed me to assess what I REALLY WANTED. I had to determine what was most important to me and not what everyone else thought was best for me. I was able to learn a lot about myself during this time. It wasn't all pleasant, but it was all needed. I looked for the lessons. **Lifestyle Success Tip: Spend time with yourself and get to know yourself better!**

I was not happy if everyone else was happy like I'd been telling myself. I wasn't fixing it all those times I thought I was. I was losing more of myself by not listening to what was being said with every lie. I had relied on counselors to guilt-trip a man who had made it clear he wasn't interested in being a husband and not really a dad that he should stay in a marriage he didn't want. I accepted that I had no one but myself to be angry at for the time spent, tears cried, and years I couldn't get back. It was me that chose to overlook the red flags, and it was me that didn't ask the questions because deep down, I already knew the answers. It was me that acted like everything was fine when it wasn't. It had been me that wanted to please people so badly that I would agree to stay in a loveless, emotionally abusive marriage because everyone loved what they thought we had, and I didn't want to disappoint them. It was me that should have left way back in 2002 when I realized I had married a stranger. I didn't want to admit it, but I had got this one wrong.

I can remember plenty of "talks," I do mean talks because we never argued. Ex would sit, agree or say things would be different and keep doing whatever he was doing. I remember plenty of talks where I would express how I felt and what I needed from him. I would tell him how I needed him to show up. It was me that thought I could fix him, get him to be the man I had believed I married. It reminds me of that scene in Sixth Sense when Bruce Willis realizes the whole time he thought he was talking to his wife, she didn't see him there. Ex never saw me. Now that I had this time to soul search, I realized I never saw him either. I didn't like who Ex was, and I had been trying for years to get him to be someone else. All the while not realizing I was losing who I was in the process. I didn't want to be that person. I wasn't the only one feeling like I wasn't good enough, so was Ex. I'd done the same thing to him he had been doing to me. Though very different motives, the results were the same. Neither one of us felt seen.

Lifestyle Success Tip: If you don't treat the trauma, you'll repeat the trauma.

Self-Love gets a bad rap. There's a narrative that says it's selfish. I say loving yourself first will help you to not only show up better for yourself but also for everyone around you.

In my sister Pearl's favorite scripture passage, Jesus replied: 'Love the Lord your God with all your heart and with all your soul and with all your mind.' This is the first and greatest commandment. And the second is like it: 'Love your neighbor as yourself.'

—Matthew 22:37-39

I didn't want my daughter to think what Ex and I had was love. I didn't want my son to think that what he witnessed was what being a husband looked like. I most definitely didn't want my kids thinking they had to be anyone besides who God had created them to be for love.

This self-love journey was showing me there was more to me. It was the ugliest, most beautiful thing. A healing process and a restorative one. I was learning how to trust who God said I was, recognize my ability to choose what was best for me, to show up more authentically. I stopped overthinking and giving validity to what people would say or think about my decisions. It was a desperate decision, I did it scared and unsure of what it would mean exactly, but it has been one of the most rewarding decisions I've ever made. I finally bet on myself and loved myself enough to trust God and then myself. Some things were about to change!

Lifestyle Tip: Sometimes, you have to let go of who you have been to become who you are meant to be.

EYES WIDE OPEN

If it wasn't happily ever after, what would it be? I wanted to be more than mom, I already knew that wasn't enough. If I wasn't going to be a wife, who was I? I sat with myself and thought about how I wanted to show up. If I wanted to laugh a lot, I would. If I wanted to say no, I would. I thought about what my family would say when I got divorced and what his family would say. What would my friends say? I decided it didn't matter. Not in the context of whether to do it or not. Aside from my sisters, who knew about some of what had gone on between Ex and I, no one knew who we were behind closed doors. That was part of why it lasted as long as it did. I was never one that wanted just a pretty picture, but I had somehow painted it anyway. Can you guess what came next?

Yup, Plan - "I Choose." I know, I can't help it. I'm a planner by nature. What I was beginning to see now was that I had options. I got to choose. I didn't have to go through the motions, and I didn't have to let life happen to me. I could be intentional about how I moved and purposeful about creating the life I wanted.

The first thing I had to decide was how long I wanted to stay in this marriage. At this point, I resolved it had been more of an arrangement for the last eight years. Still, I had to choose. I couldn't keep going on like I was. I was too aware of everything now. I knew who I was and that I wanted love. Not happily ever after as in a pretty picture or fairy tale. The vision was becoming more clear on my self-love journey. I loved myself, and it felt good. It felt freeing. I also knew that sooner or later, I would want love from someone else again, and it would not be Ex. I tested out some conversations to confirm all these thoughts I was processing weren't made up. It wasn't yet another story I was trying to convince myself was true to cope.

I told Ex I wasn't going back on what we agreed to, but I felt much like when he left the room to go downstairs all those years ago. This time though, I wasn't telling someone else. I was letting Ex know. I didn't expect him to throw his arms around me and assure me of his love for me.

I just needed to confirm there was really nothing there. There were a couple of things I was sure of now.

1. I could raise my kids alone, and they'd be the better for it.

2. I would not have to convince Ex of the divorce.

I already had the answers to the questions I never asked. It wasn't about the answers for me. I knew I wouldn't be the bitter ex-wife because I had lost the man I thought I married eight years earlier. Anyone that wanted Ex now was welcome to him. I knew God had more for me. I want to clarify that God didn't tell me to get divorced, and I'm not an advocate of divorce; it just happens to be part of my story. I was certain there was more for me, and it was clear to me I wasn't going to get to it if I stayed where I was.

I knew if I opened the door for Ex to leave, he would walk through it. For the second time in 13 years married, I was ok with that. The first time I silenced my voice and went along with what everyone thought was best for me. This time I would not. I would use my voice and do what I thought was best for everyone, myself being first. I felt relieved at this truth for both Ex and myself. I had regard for him, sure, as my kid's father, and the feeling I had most for him now was sadness. That all this time he'd been as trapped as I was. That he didn't love himself enough to leave a marriage he'd never really wanted to be in. That he wasn't brave enough to own his truth and leave. Instead, he'd try to make me so miserable that I would do it for him. Well, this was it. I loved myself enough to be the brave one and to own my truth, and I would free us both!

Our last conversation leading up to the divorce would be our last "talk," my chance to express all I felt. All the years I had felt so lonely, all the times I needed him, the lies and the truths that broke us beyond repair. His response, "I don't know what you want me to do. Nothing is going to change, so do what you have to do." I let that sit heavy over us for a couple of days and then cracked the door. "When you said to do what I have to do, did you mean divorce? Do you feel like we should just let us go?" One word and it was done..."Yea."

Next came the matter of when to tell our families. Ex had a concern about what we would tell everyone. It was this fear that kept him stuck so long. He never wanted to ever look like the bad guy. I assured him I wouldn't say anything more than "It's over." We'd tell them that we decided it was time and it's over. So we did, I would tell my mom, and he would tell his parents. Separately. We would tell everyone else in the new year. We knew when Christmas came, it would be our last together. We would wait to tell the kids until they were out of school that Summer because I wasn't sure how it would affect their schooling. He'd stay until the lease was up that next year. We'd tell the kids that mommy and daddy didn't work out. I only asked Ex one thing. I'd agree not to talk to his family or mine if he agreed that when the kids were old enough to start asking questions, he would own his part in the truth of what went on. We weren't at each other's throats, and we had just renewed our lease, so we had time. We'd just made it known where it was headed. That was the plan.

Honestly, I felt like everyone had gotten enough snippets here and there to not be too surprised. I was wrong. His family stopped talking to me, and my sisters went into full intervention mode and assembled to tell their baby sister what to do. They orchestrated an ambush where they had my nieces and nephews write me notes and tried their best to talk me into not going through with the divorce. Bless their little hearts, I know they meant well. I loved myself too much now. I would not take this one for the team. I would no longer worry about what made everyone feel better or more comfortable. I would do what was best for myself, my children and Ex.

The plan didn't work out as intended. When Ex said he wanted to tell the kids sooner, file the paperwork and move out by March, we adjusted and planned accordingly. We were both talking to other people by now, and I was just as ready to move forward. Ready to move on with a new love for self and in great expectation of more. As far as I knew at the time, there were no secrets, no more lies and we were done. It had been over for a long time, but now we could both finally walk in that truth. I was no longer trying to fix it. Ex no longer had to pretend. It was a weight lifted from both of us.

Lifestyle Success Tip: Sometimes, the best way to get something to work is to stop trying to fix it.

Now with my eyes wide open, I was about to find out that happily ever after was within me and a lifelong journey I was living out in real-time. **Lifestyle Success Tip: Don't let life change you. Choose to change your life.**

Reflection

Write a "thank you" letter to yourself and
express how you're going to show up better.

Dear ME, Thank you for _____

_____

_____

_____

_____

_____

_____

_____

_____

_____

_____

5

SUPERWOMAN

I questioned myself so many times in life. Why did I stay so long in a marriage based on continuous lies, neglect, emotional manipulation and the absence of love? As weak as it made me feel, I stayed and told myself it was strength. I was enduring. I was being strong and sticking it out. Not giving up. I thought about my mom, my sisters. I grew up in a family of superwomen! The females far outranked the males, and the females always called the shots. My mom, Queen Bee, outranked us all. I would already be living in Paris if I had saved a nickel every time I heard my dad say, "Well, Jamie, that's your mother." She could do no wrong. I'd plead with him to speak up. I ask why he just went along with whatever she said. If we were all in the living room telling stories and laughing (because that was a typical day in life before the internet), my mom would be the one to break it up because she was tired and ready to go to bed. "Come on, Joe, I'm ready for bed." I never understood why he had to go when she was the one tired. Pearl told me after I was married. It makes perfect sense now. Sex really is the best sleep medicine. No wonder my dad jumped to his feet and followed. Ok, mom, respect!

My dad was born and raised in North Carolina and held onto his southern hospitality and charm when he moved north to New Jersey. It wasn't hard for him to treat my mom like a queen. I don't recall my mom ever driving my dad. She drove on her own, but she would not be playing chauffeur if he was in the car. It annoyed him to see my boyfriend in the passenger seat of my car. Whatever my mom said went. If I wanted to go to the mall, the movies or spend the night out, it was a yes from my dad, unless it was a no from my mom. "It's fine with me, but go ask your mother." He was the man of the house, so I couldn't understand why he didn't have the last say. I realize now he was teaching me without teaching me, what it was like to lead. **Lifestyle Success Tip: The best leaders are the ones that serve.**

My mom is the strongest woman I know, her resilience after losing her only son, her favorite aunt, her father, her mother, her husband of over 40 Years, her sister and her firstborn daughter. She keeps going, and she keeps trusting God. I looked to her for what to do and what not to do. What I loved I mimicked, and what I didn't love, I made a conscious effort not to repeat. I sometimes have to shake my head as I hear myself say the same things my mom said growing up. "Are their parents going to be home?" "Make sure you get those dishes out the sink." "Get in here and clean this mess up!" "If I go in there and find it, you're in trouble."

Although we are extremely close now, my mom and I were not as close while I was growing up. I spent a lot of time with my sister, Pearl, who I considered a second mom. My mom had not been thrilled about getting pregnant at 36, seven years after having what she thought was her last child. I heard the story more than once growing up about how she had cried and cried about the pregnancy and how my dad had assured her it would be ok. Combine that information with hearing about how she suffered from Postpartum Depression. I simply thought even after carrying me for nine months, she still had not wanted me. I didn't understand at the time that Postpartum Depression happens to 1 in 9 new moms and was not something she could control.

I believed the story I put together for quite some time. It resulted in me drawing closer to my sister, who always had me with her and my dad, who had wanted me. Creating a distance between my mom and I. While she was being her typical mom self and fussing about things moms fuss about, I always took it a little more personally because, in my mind, she hadn't really wanted me anyway. *Lifestyle Success Tip: Be careful when you are talking around children. They are listening.*

I remember feeling like my mom must have forgotten what being a teenager was like during my teenage years. It didn't seem she could relate to me at all. Kind of like how my daughter feels now (right back at me). Her teenage years had been a little different, having eloped with my dad at the age of 16 and had my sister by the age of 17 (nope, she wasn't pregnant first). I hadn't considered the impact that had on her teenage years, if you can even call them that. I just noted that she didn't seem to understand fun, teenage love, the stress of high school or me hanging out with friends. She couldn't understand why if I'd just spent all day in school with my bestie, we still had so much to talk about on the phone when we got home. So many telephone cords ripped out the wall because I was under the covers still talking on the phone after I should have been off by 10 pm. Ahh, fun times...in hindsight of course!

Anyway, at one point in my life, I began praying that my mom would have joy. She didn't laugh as hard as the rest of us, and she would complain we were too loud when my sisters and I were all standing around cracking each other up. "Do y'all have to laugh so loud? How can you even hear each other?!" "Stop yelling." A complete party pooper. If you wanted someone to rain on your parade, don't worry, she was going to do it. I remember that annoyed me so much because my dad was quite the opposite, the fun one, full of laughs and the life of the party.

Even when I didn't agree with my mom, I looked to her. I knew she set the mood and controlled the atmosphere. I knew my mom was the one handling things. She instilled this same strength and dominance in my sisters and I. Without realizing it, I was looking up to her for the example to follow. She is my superhero, my Superwoman. There are only a couple of times I can remember her breaking character and how it impacted me each time she did...

The first time I can remember is in the car pulling off from visiting my brother's gravesite. My mother broke down crying, kicking the floor of the car, "my son! my son!" Me being so young at the time, I remember watching from the backseat and seeing a tear roll down my dad's cheek. I was crying now, so upset that she had made him cry. I couldn't understand why she had to break down like that. We'd all done so well at the site, now she had upset us all. Why?! I didn't connect the two until now, but the second time would be when the doctor came out and let us know they couldn't remove the cancer from my sister's lung like they thought they could.

I remember my mom breaking down again, full distress mode. My sister had cancer, but she wasn't dead. Once again, we're all trying to be strong and take in this horrific news. We are all trying to hold it together, and here she was getting ready to upset us all. I yelled at her, "Stop it. You're acting like he said she died. She's still here!" I know that was pretty harsh. I have since apologized to her for that. I remember these two instances so vividly because they were the few times I saw my mom without her cape. Queen Bee, the strong one. The one that held us down. Why was that so upsetting to me? Why wasn't it okay for her to cry? Why wasn't it okay for her to be upset that she had lost her only son and that this surgeon had just told her she wouldn't have her first born daughter much longer? I thought about this, and it was because she is my symbol of strength. She's the one that always held it together. She was the reason I knew I could be strong. But if she wasn't, if she couldn't do it. What did that mean for me?

It wasn't until I was older, married to Ex and with my own children that I understood her a little better. Having my daughter taught me the depths of love. This tiny person I almost never had, had shown up and changed my world. I can't imagine the loss of a child, but I have to believe it is the most unimaginable pain that no parent should ever bear.

I thought about how that pain could change a person, how maybe you wouldn't laugh as much. And how maybe if you held in the hurt and the pain, you would no doubt have days where you couldn't hold it in anymore, and you'd cry, kick and scream.

I know the source of the Lord is our strength, but somehow someone decided to put the unbearable burden of strength on black women to be a close second. This is what is portrayed, and this is the expectation that is silently or sometimes audibly communicated. To set the atmosphere, hold it down, and keep it together so that everyone else can. **Lifestyle Success Tip: Allow yourself to cry.**

Dear Mom,

Thank you for always playing the part. I know it was not easy. I know that you held in way too much so that we could see strength and be strong ourselves. You have experienced pain no mother should ever know. Forgive me for ever taking you for granted. Thank you for taking such good care of our family and ensuring we always had more than enough. Thank you for letting dad shine even when it made you look like the bad guy. Thank you for doing your best to love us just right and give us what you knew we needed. I'm so happy you've found joy and your laugh makes my heart so warm. Thank you for trusting Pearl with me. Though she played a big part, she could never replace you. I see how you've grown, and I'm proud of you. You are still my hero. I so enjoy our time spent together and love our talks, our laughs, shared meals and hugs. I love that you have been there for me and my family (Reesie too). I am forever grateful for how much you mean to each of us. I love you beyond measure, and I hope I make you proud!

Your baby girl,
Jamie

SUPERWOMEN

I'm sharing this story about my mom to encourage you not to put unnecessary pressure on yourself, trying to do the most and all the things. When your body, mind and spirit need it, rest. Avoid burnout and creating overwhelm for yourself. Being the planner I am, I am always making lists. The overwhelming feeling comes in when I know good and well I can't do in the time I have during the day, even half of what I put on my list to do. So I create this place of overwhelm just by creating this massive list and never completing it. The stress of all these things I had to get done! Instead, I try now to be more realistic about the time I have and the rest I know I will need in-between. It's also a good idea to be realistic about what really has to get done instead of what would be nice to get done. **Lifestyle Success Tip: Plan your day so that you can get the most out of it, not the most done.**

I encourage you also to not just embrace self-love and think about how you want to show up and who you want to be. Leave time to grow into the areas you are not familiar with or haven't identified. Leave room for where God wants to lead you that He hasn't shown you yet. Though you don't see it, know that wherever it is, His plans are for good, to give you a future and hope. Allow yourself to step into new spaces and become brand new if that's what it takes, stay well-rested and ready.

This is what makes you super! That is our superpower as women, that we can continually evolve, that we can continually get better and better, that we can multitask and do so many things well. Set intention and purpose behind what you do and make sure that you love yourself enough to cultivate happiness, peace and serve your physical, emotional and mental well-being.

Ok, maybe a little random, but thinking about how super we are. Can we talk about our bodies real quick? Our amazing bodies that can go up and down the scale, these amazing bodies, some of which have birth children, some of which have survived, like mine being cut deep and open wide to bring life into the world. Your amazing body that you need to love enough to embrace it for being the one body you get! Accept it because it's going to be what takes you on this journey, this journey of self-love, purpose and lifestyle success! Get the sleep you need, eat what's good for you and treat yourself to some things that aren't so good for you. If one day you want that chocolate Oreo milkshake, then have it. You'll still be super and you are always amazing.

To all my superwomen out there, that includes YOU holding this book...break down whenever you need to to get the release you need to build yourself back up. Allow yourself to feel everything you need to feel, sad, mad, tired, exhausted, joy, happiness and love, ALL OF IT! If you just need that space, a nap, or a break, TAKE IT! I know it feels like it won't get done if you don't do it, and I see you burning yourself out trying to do it all. While you're taking care of everyone else, who's taking care of you? You do not have to be a superwoman all of the time. Give yourself permission to take off your cape, rest your crown and breathe. Do or don't do whatever it is you need to for YOU.

Reflection

What would it feel like for you to take
off your cape and rest your crown?

Taking off my cape would make me feel_____

_____

_____

_____

_____

_____

_____

_____

_____

_____

_____

_____

PART II

How It's Going

6

I CHOOSE HAPPY

It's a beautiful thing when you realize you have choices. You get to choose who you will be and how you will show up. I have a quote framed on the wall behind me right now as I write this that reads, "People are as happy as they choose to be." - Abraham Lincoln. It serves as a two-fold reminder that 1. I get to choose happy and 2. I'm not responsible for anyone else's. There is power in getting to choose. I'm not talking about the feeling so much as the state of being.

Happy

1. Feeling or showing pleasure or contentment.
2. Fortunate and convenient.

Happiness

The state of being happy.

I was in a dark place for a long time, trying to make someone happy so that they would love me. My darkest days have made choosing happy easier. Like me, you get to choose happy over anxiety if your job starts doing layoffs. You get to choose to be content with whatever door God opens and whatever door He chooses to close. You get to choose to focus on how fortunate you are to have a job, even if the people on that job work your last nerve. You get to choose! I had to choose not to stress over uncertainty and instead remind myself that God hasn't failed me yet and won't start now. Choosing happy was forgiving Ex and releasing the hurt, resentment and disappointment so that I could open myself up to love again. Hello somebody! Can you pause and clap it up for THAT part?! Thanks, Sis!

Happiness is more than that feeling you get when you've somehow managed to get 15 minutes alone to yourself. Happiness is a mindset. It is choosing to believe a new truth. You get to create your own reality by the habits you keep and the stories you tell yourself. Your habits will determine your lifestyle. For so long, I told myself that I wasn't good enough. I did this by consistently striving for perfection.

Lifestyle Success Tip: There is no perfect! If you're going to strive, strive to be better.

Choosing happy is not a one-time thing. It is a higher habit that you incorporate into your everyday routine until it becomes who you are. When you start telling yourself that it's a bad day, it will be. Instead, choose to look for joy. Start a daily gratitude practice. Remember that thank you makes room for more. Be it positive energy or negative energy, and you will attract whichever you choose to focus on. I look for at least five things that I'm thankful for every day. This way, come what may throughout my day, I know there is some joy I can look to. If you look for joy, you'll find it. You get to choose how you want to use your voice.

Choose to speak up or choose silence when it's the better option. I found so much freedom in choosing not to speak about my divorce when it was happening. I wanted to focus on my journey and the next season in my life and the changes it would bring. I'd already given enough energy to the relationship. I knew talking about it when it was over was not going to generate any positivity. Besides, Ex and I had an agreement. I was being intentional about attracting what I wanted more of in my life. You will find power in choosing for yourself. In my case, after announcing the divorce, people put their own stories together. I found out four years later that Ex had helped encourage a false narrative. Even when it was all said and done, and I'd held up my end of not talking about it, he still felt the need to tell lies. Till this day, people believe a completely different narrative from my truth. I say this to say that choosing happy won't always come easy.

The lies were no surprise, of course, but I was very disappointed. I was upset that my sister Pearl was one of the people who believed many of those lies. The distance between us her last year here on earth hadn't been just because I decided to get a divorce, but she had been fed lies as to why the divorce was happening. There was no clearing it up because she was dead. Nothing I could do to change that, so I forgave Ex once again. I let him know I knew about the stories he'd led people to believe so that he could play the victim. I let him know how disappointed I was that he'd been the cause of the distance between my sister and I the last year I had to spend with her. I chose to use my voice, to speak my truth and then I chose to let it go. **Lifestyle Success Tip: People are going to talk, let them.**

Whenever possible, choose positivity and peace. Don't let what people may say or think dictate how you move. You feel me? Good. People can try to steal your joy, but remember, they can only do that if you let them. You choose!

Choose to be the energy you want to attract. Life can appear to just happen when you're not deliberate about your choices. One of the best choices you'll ever make is to choose

114

to seek God first in all you do, through prayer and His Word. This will assure that your steps are ordered and help to set intention and purpose for your life. When you are mindful of who you are and Whose you are, choosing those things that serve you best will become a lot easier. Choose faith over fear, community over competition, peace over pride, love over lies and positive vibes over negativity. **Lifestyle Success Tip: Not choosing is choosing.**

If you don't make deliberate choices, you get stuck with the default. I had to work really hard to shift my mindset from a fixed one to a growth one. To go from believing I had to have a plan for every scenario life would throw at me, to believing I get to choose what scenario I want for my life.

Circumstances will come up, and situations will arise. We get to choose how much we let them impact who we are and how we show up for ourselves and others. Remember when I shared my bankruptcy experience with you? I could have chosen to panic and to go about my days frantic over what I couldn't control. Instead, by the grace of God, I chose to protect my peace and trust that God was working it out for my good. I had to be purposeful about finding joy in each day by remembering God was meeting my needs daily. I chose to focus on the fact that my family woke up with a roof still over their heads, had enough to eat, and I was able to show up for my children. Literally choosing happy one day at a time when tomorrow held so much uncertainty.

Even today, people try to convince me I'm not as happy as I say I am. This is because they haven't asserted their authority to choose. It's hard to understand something you haven't personally experienced. I get it. This idea of getting to choose may sound unrealistic to you. Maybe you're thinking easier said than done. It is. I am not saying it will always be easy. I am saying it will always be worth it! You get to choose if you will focus on the fact that you have everything you need today or worry about the fact that you don't know what tomorrow will bring. You get to choose happy!

"I know that there is nothing better for people than to be happy and to do good while they live."

— Ecclesiastes 3:12

I AM ENOUGH

Enough. I wrote that on a piece of paper and got it along my wrist for my first tattoo. It is a truth I need to make sure I always remember. This truth allows me to simply BE. I don't have to overthink why I am the way I am and if that is good enough. I don't need titles or roles to define me. Before I was "wife" or "mom", I was Jamie. I was enough then, and I am enough now. I stopped looking for excuses as to why my no is a no. Most importantly, I no longer feel like I have to validate who I am or justify my actions. No more wearing my hair a certain way because of what the people at work might say. Shaved sides and loc's it is! I first wanted my hair in loc's during my twenties and let someone talk me out of it. I wasn't confident enough to stand by what I wanted for MY hair. No more! I found my voice and am going to live my best life using it. I heard references about personal boundaries over the years but had never set them. Now I have. Not only should you set personal boundaries, but be sure to respect and honor them. You set the example for others to respect and honor them as well. **Lifestyle Success Tip: Being intentional about what you want, increases your chances of getting it.**

It's been a journey to get here, I can remember the feeling of not wanting to lose my newfound freedom from people's opinions and the confidence I found in speaking up for what I really wanted. I was learning to no longer shrink myself to make others comfortable. I promised myself to no longer deny myself a good laugh or a good cry. I committed to honoring my children by loving myself first and filling my cup so that I could give them my best and not the overwhelmed, burnt-out scraps of what was left after trying to cater to everyone else first. I took ownership of my choices and communicated my needs. This was not about being selfish. This was about being my BEST!

I would love and trust God first, and then I would love and trust myself. I identified my top 5 personal core values...

- Self-Love
- Freedom
- Happiness
- Purpose
- Peace

These are the things that are most important to me. These are values that help me when making decisions, weighing my options and assessing opportunities. I ask myself does it align with my core values? This is how I can assure that my state of being can be so happy most of the time. I choose to align myself with things that are most important and bring me joy. There is no perfectionism in enough, though there is an appreciation for progress and growth. I still have days when I doubt myself or find myself striving for perfection. It happened during the writing of this book. My author coach Nikkie Pryce asked me how the book was coming along. The disappointment on my face was obvious, and I could feel the tears flooding my eyes. I had not reached my weekly goal of 70 pages but instead had only 65. She celebrated me, clapped it up on the screen of our Zoom call and asked why I was having such a hard time celebrating myself. Why? Because 65 wasn't 70, I hadn't met my goal.

Maybe it was writing about perfectionism for the past week or that this writing process has applied pressure I had not anticipated. That pressure had brought me right back to that perfectionist that had to get it just right, or it was wrong.

My coach reminded me that just a week prior and three years prior to that, I had zero pages written. Boom! An instant perspective shift I wish I could take credit for. I share that to show that I have my days when I get in my head and forget that I am enough. I feel disappointed and sad. The growth is that I don't stay in that place for long. I can shift perspective, or in this case, because I've been intentional about who I surround myself with, I am never far from someone that can remind me and nudge me toward the truth. My coach was right!!! I had zero pages and no clue how to start a book, and now I had 65 pages of my book written! AYYYEEE!!! I chose to celebrate that instead of feeling disappointed about being 5 pages short of 70. **Lifestyle Success Tip: Keep things in perspective. Perfectionism will only steal your joy.**

Another thing that will steal your joy is comparison, which the internet and social media have strongly influenced the increase of. From Likes, to Follows, to OnlyFans (yikes). Photoshop and filters encourage what they perceive to be the perfect features. It's no wonder the plastic surgery industry has seen such an uptick. I'm learning to appreciate my body. It is the only one I have, after all. I stopped second-guessing myself and devaluing myself. I had to stop thinking my lack of a college degree made me less than. A little trick I do to avoid comparing and anxiety creeping in. I get excited about volunteering first! Pick me! Pick me! Not because I'm so confident and ready, but because I won't compare my response or answer to the person who came before me. You're welcome, hope that helps! Think about ways you can show appreciation for who you are today? You are enough to take the leap, to do it scared and trust God on the way up!

Written 12/7/2015 @5:17 am - Enough

Not black enough. Tell that to the store clerk that failed to return a smile. She followed me around from isle to isle. Then there was that other woman who made me mad, moving her purse to her other shoulder as if I wanted something she had. When I stand to give my opinion, before I can make an audible sound, there will be someone already telling me to "calm down"

I could point to my ancestry instead, what little of it I know. Just look at me..you see the natural curve in my hips and the fullness of my lips

ENOUGH.

Not light enough, not dark enough. Like anyone had a choice they can take credit for. Where was I the "Black" Friday you went, shopped and selected your complexion to add to your cart!?!?! I am in the skin I was born in.

ENOUGH.

Not fast enough. I don't have to be picked first or even at all to know my value. I know my worth. Others running may no doubt pass me by while going for the "win", but I've learned that the race is not given to the swift but to the ones that endure till the end

ENOUGH.

Not smart enough. God grants wisdom to those that ask Him, and I am smart enough to trust Him and know some things...I simply don't know. A fool is the one who thinks they know it all.

ENOUGH.

Not loved enough. Even if I was the only soul on the planet, God would have sent His one and only begotten son to die for my sins. That's my foundation. That is where my love story begins

ENOUGH.

Not short or tall enough. Well, how about when I can finally get on, it's spinning so fierce my stomach's all scrambled inside, now I'm nauseous and yelling, please stop the ride! Everything is not for me and some rides I've simply outgrown.

ENOUGH.

The list can go on and on with the lies I'd told myself or been told over time. Somewhere along MY life's journey, I took a look at my experiences, trials, successes and failures, I made time to focus inward on "me". I've grown, I've learned, and now I embrace and love what I see.

For "ME" I make no apology. For anyone who doesn't recognize or choose to see ME, I no longer make that concern of mine. I don't focus on such things. My truth will remain...

I AM ENOUGH.

FREE TO BE

Of all of my core values, I definitely favor freedom. Thus another tattoo I designed on the inside of my upper arm that reads FREE inside of a cross. I love it because it can mean so many things. But if I had to say one thing, it's that I am free to BE!

Free

1. Not under the control or in the power of another; able to act or be done as one wishes.
2. Not or no longer confined or imprisoned.

Freedom

The power or right to act, speak or think as one wants without hindrance or restraint.

Having spent so much of my life in a self-imposed prison of perfection, control, fear, and people-pleasing the freedom to make mistakes, trust the process, do things scared and be free from the opinion of others was quite liberating. It's a never-ending journey to maintain and sustain that freedom. I don't want to give you the impression that there is a one-time fix. The higher habits I cultivated of self-love, surrender, boundaries and more, help tremendously. The mind is the most powerful tool we have outside of prayer. I have to remind myself that I'm striving for progress and not perfection when I find myself sitting too long and overthinking something as simple as a post on Instagram.

The tendency for perfection is still there, and my anxiety is never too far away. BUT I have the tools now. I know how to hit reset in my mind and move past the moment or even sometimes navigate through it. I still have triggers from my years of feeling like I wasn't heard. My husband will tell you I can't stand repeating myself, a simple "What did you say about "ABC" again?" will turn into a lengthy conversation about him not listening to me, rather than a short answer. There is baggage to unpack there that I brought with me from my first marriage to Ex. It's a trigger, and I have to work consciously to not let it be a barrier in our relationship. I'm aware of it, I own it and I have communicated it clearly. I'm recalling the feeling that what I said didn't matter enough to care to listen. That's the freedom to be able to recognize that, speak to it and be ok that I'm still a work in progress. That freedom is what I want you to experience. You are not striving for perfection, only better, and better, and better!

You don't have to suppress feelings, pretend and build up walls. I'm in a very good season in my life, and I have a lot of good days, glory to God. I'm also free to have not-so-good ones. I don't have those nearly as much as I used to, because I can encourage myself and choose happy, but I have them, and only a perfectionist mindset would feel like that was not ok. Embrace your freedom to be. There were so many emotions I suppressed that resurfaced in the process of writing this book. I had not permitted myself to feel the full range I was created to express. Allow yourself to feel. Remember that you get to choose and that what you feed will grow. Freedom is laughing as much and hard as you want and crying as much and hard as you need to. You are free to be your true authentic self. There may be times you code switch at work because you don't want to be labeled the angry black woman. You are still free to flip that switch and give me a "YAAASSS Sis. I see YOU!" as well! The freedom of authenticity isn't about being one way. It is about being your way.

God created you to be free in Him. Every time I passed the mic, I locked myself away because I didn't want to "talk too much". I've always been a talker. It's been on every report card since kindergarten. "Jamie is a pleasure to have in class but a little too social.", "Jamie is a pleasure to have in class but talks too much to her peers." Talking just comes naturally to me, connecting with people and striking up conversations. It is what I did every time they changed my seat, which was quite a lot. When you hear you talk too much all your life, you eventually start to believe the narrative. I would start incorporating it in conversations, "I know I'm probably talking too much." or "I'll stop, I don't want to talk too much." How ironic, people pay me now to talk, and I get to connect with amazing people all over the world and strike up conversations. Isn't that something! I tell that little back story to encourage you to be free to be exactly who you are. Don't embrace someone else's narrative about you. Be your own narrative. You are free to create it and tell your own story. **Lifestyle Success Tip: If you don't tell your story, someone will tell it for you.**

I gave a lot of energy to what people would think, which manifested as anxiety and I became extremely indecisive. No matter if I was crystal clear on what I wanted, I would ask someone else what they thought was best. Which one should I wear? Do you think this is too much? I really want this, but whatever you want is fine. Always scared to make a decision without asking for buy-in or having someone else make the decision for me. Only then would I own it as my own and feel good about it. I don't discourage wise counsel. There is a definite benefit to asking someone who has already been where you're going for directions or about what that experience was for them. I want you to keep a couple of things in mind, though...

1. Their way may be one of many ways to get there, explore your options.
2. Their experience is going to be based on their choices and may be influenced by their childhood conditioning, which makes their experience different from yours.

Take note and get to know yourself enough to take what will serve you and leave what won't. I often quote

Shakespeare to my clients, "To thy own self be true." Your freedom to be, is in learning about yourself and checking in with yourself often so that you can trust yourself enough to make the choices you know are best for you. **Lifestyle Success Tip: Date yourself, schedule quality alone time to check in with yourself at least once a week.**

Stay in step with the vision God has shown you for your life, and align with your core values. Come out from under the weight of getting it wrong. Silence the anxious voice in your head that wants to have you question yourself and enable your freedom to be. Own your truth, your emotions, your narrative and your story. We all get one life to live. Live your life in the freedom to be who God created you to be!

Reflection

Reflect on what Happiness is to you.
How can you be more intentional about choosing it?

Happiness to me is _____

_____

_____

_____

_____

_____

_____

_____

_____

_____

_____

7

KNOW, LIKE, TRUST

In order to follow someone, you have to trust them. This is a known marketing principle I've learned in business that says before a person will purchase from you, they need to "Know, Like and Trust" you. I've found that holds true in my personal life too. Communication is a major component of any relationship as it helps to build a sense of security and trust (Know, Like, Trust). If you don't trust what a person tells you, it will be very hard to build a safe and secure foundation. It will be impossible to build anything without communication. I wish I had understood this earlier in life. It would have saved me a lot of time, planning, wishing and hoping. Know, Like, Trust is particularly important when it comes to your relationship with God, the most important relationship you will have. Do you know God? Not about Him, but know Him? I knew God most of my life, and I liked Him too. He was a constant, someone I knew wouldn't leave and wouldn't change. What I didn't do, was always trust Him. Why? Because even though I had always been around Him and I had spoken to Him, I had gotten out of the practice of spending quality time communicating with Him.

During my self-love journey, I found out God spoke all the time! I just hadn't been listening enough to really hear Him. Earnest prayer and reading His Word has grown our relationship to one I know, like and trust.

"Those who know your name trust you because you have not abandoned any who seek you, Lord."

— Psalm 9:1

Lifestyle Success Tip: Communication is two-way. Spend just as much time listening as you do talking, if not more!

My relationship with myself grew as well. The more I spent time with myself, communicating how I felt, what I needed, learning who I really was, the more I learned to know, like and trust myself. Now, like most relationships, you are not going to like EVERYTHING about the person. You'll learn there are some things about yourself you don't like. I discovered conversations that weren't sitting well with me. Why was I telling myself I wasn't lovable? Why had I believed myself when I said I wasn't good enough. I had to look at myself and ask myself some tough questions. What was it that made me think I could change people, fix people? There's a popular quote that hits differently when you've been through a few things.

"When people show you who they are, believe them the first time."

— Maya Angelou

I had to get to know myself and understand why I was such a people-pleaser. The truth was I wanted to feel accepted, and the anxiety and fear came from not wanting to be rejected. That may sound like I said the same thing two different ways, but I didn't. Wanting to be accepted may sound like, "Hey, do you mind if I join you?" Where not wanting to be rejected sounds like, "Hey, tell me what I have to do to join you." Subtle, but the difference is the desperation in the latter. I am not absolutely sure that I can pinpoint the beginning of where that fear came from, but I remember a time in elementary school when I found out from my friend that the moms stood around and talked about me. They'd said I was "street-smart" because I had older sisters. They didn't want my friends to spend so much time with me.

My friend was hoping that we'd still get to play together. I was surprised to hear the moms talked about me to each other. I remember trying to understand what they meant by "street-smart." We couldn't ask, of course, because then they would know my friend had been up in grown folk's business. The conclusion was that whatever it meant, they thought I wasn't good enough to play with their daughters, my very best friends.

A spirit of inferiority set in. I started watching my grades more closely and comparing them to others. I tried to say the right things and not the wrong ones, even though I wasn't quite sure what those were. I had just been me, and this time was the first time that I can remember that 'me', wasn't good enough. I had been rejected, and now I desperately wanted to be liked. When you operate out of fear, you can't always be trusted. You may compromise your values, self-respect and self-worth. You do anything to be loved, anything to not be on the outside looking in. Once trust is broken, you won't be liked, because no one likes a liar.

I was operating in fear most of my life, of being rejected, of dying and of my parents losing another child, fear of dying before my bucket list was checked off, of not having happily ever after, of disappointing my family, of disappointing God. I lost sleep, and I lost weight. I was overly emotional, very defensive, and through it all, something happened that it never occurred for me to be afraid of, I lost myself. The reality was it wasn't the marriage relationship I needed a plan for fixing all those years. It was my relationship with myself.

I didn't know myself enough to like or trust me. What I did think I knew, I had heard from someone else. I was pretty, I was too talkative, street smart, my lips were too big, I sounded too "white," I had nice eyes, I laughed too much, I had a nice smile, I wasn't as smart as my friends, and my long hair made me assumed to be stuck up. While I could have focused on the "good," I chose to focus on the "bad."

The beauty in spending time with myself and focusing inward was those hard conversations and memories I had to reflect on showed me a lot. I saw ME. I had been presented with options, and I made choices. There had been times I chose to believe a thing true that had now proven false. I had gotten to play with my friends regardless of what their moms thought, my lips hadn't changed, but once I started kissing, I figured out they weren't so bad. Some of those friends I thought were smarter were making their own mistakes. I had to adjust my narrative. If those truths were no longer true, what else wasn't? I had to reflect on the past almost 18 years with Ex and own that I went in with my eyes wide shut. I had to own that if I want to be happy, I would be the one to make that happen. I survived losing my brother, being raped, losing my daddy, losing the perfect I'd tried to be, the man I thought I'd married and the happily ever after I'd always wanted.

I lost my home and credit score, bankruptcy and my oldest sister to freakin Cancer. I was still standing, barely, but I was standing, and for the first time in a long time, I was proud of that! My self-talk improved. I was resilient! I had been through things that some people didn't see their way out of. I took time to celebrate my victories and thanked God for the favor and grace that was apparent in and throughout my life. I got on the same page with God about who He said I was. I was fearlessly and wonderfully made. I am a child of the Most High God! As I transformed my narrative and got to know the woman I was becoming, I embraced my new truths, I learned to trust myself. **Lifestyle Success Tip: Get to know, like and trust yourself.**

CULTIVATE YOUR CIRCLE

It is so important to protect your peace. One of the ways you do this is by cultivating your circle. Surround yourself with like-minded people that will embrace you for YOU, inspire growth and challenge you never to settle. Cultivate a circle that will help you to see the greatness in you. A circle that will call you out and go to bat for you. I need you to know that depending on the season you are in, this circle will change. I need you to be ok with that. We are creatures of habit, and it is easy to get used to people, places and things. No matter if they are serving you well or not. This journey of self-love, happiness and purpose is meant to serve you well. There will be times when you will have to choose along the way to let go of the things that don't add value and serve you well. Even when that involves people and means letting go and moving on. Sometimes this will come easy. Other times not. **Lifestyle Success Tip: Everyone isn't meant to go with you.**

I have my ride or dies, some that go back as far as the babysitter days, and I have my passerby's that showed up to be what I needed in a season. You may already be assessing your circle in your head. Good! What I want you to resolve from this is to be ok either way they fall. Do not feel obligated to keep relationships with people to spare their feelings or because of time and convenience. Resist overthinking why some relationships don't last. This includes associates, friends, family and even social media connections.

Don't hesitate to block people and unfollow. You decide your vibe and tribe! You may need to have some courageous conversations to put an end to toxic relationships, and sometimes relationships will simply dwindle away as you step further into your next season. Appreciate everyone for the part they play in your story. Likewise, the part you play in theirs. You may have some people that are just there to grow from you and some that are there to pour into you. Sometimes there is great exchange, and other times, you can't even remember how or why you connected with this person in the first place.

Invest in yourself so you can add value to the circles you occupy. Assess if you build up and encourage. Are you adding value and bringing good energy? The saying is we become who we spend the most time with. While I'm not sure that is entirely true, I will say that if you are not mindful about the company you keep you may find that you stay somewhere you're not meant to be for too long. Be careful not to surround yourself with people who aren't looking to grow or go where your purpose is calling you. The conversations may start to feel strained or become fewer and far between. This will happen as you lean into your self-love journey and pursue your purpose. I want you to remember what you are reading right now and don't overthink what you may have said or done wrong. Don't stress if they think you're acting funny or ask why they haven't called. It may be that the extra time you've taken to invest in yourself has created a much-needed space. **Lifestyle Success Tip: You may think you know what you want, but God will always give you what you need.**

Let the relationships that fall away go and appreciate what you were able to gain from them for the season you had them. Those gaps may hurt a little at the time, but will be filled with people who are meant to help and support you in your next season. Be purposeful about avoiding gossip and negative energy, clearly communicate your boundaries and always stay open to what inevitable change will bring out and transform in you.

People can't always give what you give, don't take it personally. Don't be mean, get jealous, compare or be easily offended. Most of the time, it's not about you. Be your own bestie and biggest cheerleader. Try not to get caught up in who isn't supporting you that you thought would. You will be surprised at the people watching you and who will come through for you on the way. People are assigned to you, some for a lifetime, some in passing and some only for a season.

"If you want to go fast, go alone; but if you want to go far, go together."

—African Proverb

TRUST YOUR PROCESS

Having learned to trust God for the plans He has for me, and learning to trust myself more and more as I lean on the Lord through my journey, also meant learning to trust my process. As much as I would love for God to take me from open door to open door, I know that the real victory takes place in the hallway. Every day I pray, "Dear God, open and shut doors according to your purpose and will for my life."

The hallway between each open and shut door is the process.

The process will be different for everyone. I've learned to trust it though it may challenge me, may frustrate me, may invite my anxiety back and worry me. It will, without a doubt, grow me and prepare me for greater. I've learned to trust my process because I know I win in the end. Trusting my process, this book being an example, has also taught me that I'm already winning along the way. **Lifestyle Success Tip: Sis, you're already winning!**

You get better in the hallway. Your journey, the process, is going to stretch you. It will require you to do things you have not done before, which may be scary. I remember when I started my blog and set up the Instagram account. I had no intention of showing my face. I hadn't shown it on my personal account because it was public, and I didn't want strangers seeing me. Then the idea of the blog came to me, and I had to get over my beef with social media and embrace it for the good that could come of it. If people were clearly spending their time on it, I would be the change I wanted to see. I would give them some inspiration to apply to their lives, and I would do that from a behind-the-scenes approach that felt safe, like not showing my face. Blog post and quotes. I imagine God laughed and thought that was cute considering the plans He had for me (Jeremiah 11:29). I imagine He thought this girl really has no idea what I'm about to do in her life. I wasn't dreaming big enough yet.

The process was one of the small steps to overcome the anxiety of showing my face and people having something negative to say. You see, even when I know I am enough and I choose happy, the voice is still there, reminding me of the narrative I believed for such a long time. When you find those old voices creeping up, especially when you're about to make a move, embrace another level on your journey and welcome a new process...anxiety, fear and doubt will come and attempt to prevent you from winning, to block your blessing and to delay your breakthrough. If you can remember their intent, you will be more likely to put them in their place. My process is teaching me consistency, to prioritize the vision and manage my time and show up. Now when I hear those voices, I get excited. I know they are only there to stop me, which means it's about to be GOOD!

My purpose requires me to not only show my face, but God has shown me a vision of me speaking on stage and signing books. WHOA God, slow down! Too much, too fast! I wasn't ready when I first saw it. I realize it wasn't for right then. There would be a process to get here. I had to trust my process through the small steps like opening up to share online and the bigger ones like embracing that it's not about me but the women I am meant to reach and impact. Let me say that again because I want to make sure you caught that. IT'S NOT

ABOUT ME! It's about each soulmate client (as my coach Kelly J. calls them) that I've helped and will help through my story and with my gifts. Each person assigned to me that I cross paths with. It is about YOU holding this book right now to know that your story matters! Your journey and your process matter because someone needs what you have. You have people assigned to you that are either where you were or where you are that will need to hear your process. They will need to hear your story to get them to their next level of greatness. They will need to know like I'm about to tell you, it gets better! *Lifestyle Success Tip: Sis, it gets better!*

My journey may look different than yours, but the process is very much the same. My process has victories and challenges designed just for me to become who God needs me to be for His will for my life, my family, and the women whose lives I am meant to impact. Your process, like mine, is designed to get you to where God intends for you to be in His will and live according to the purpose He created you for. To serve the people assigned to you that cross your path. It may be a little as a smile or as big as a life transformational coaching course. I have to trust my process to get me to my next open door. Trust that yours is designed to do the same. God has a vision for your life. If He's shared it with you, trust your process will get you there. Lean into the lessons in the hallway, confront fears, overcome anxiety and build the confidence you need for your next open door. Be obedient as not to delay your own or anyone else's breakthrough. **Lifestyle Success Tip: Resist the urge to compare. It will only distract you.**

Your process is designed especially for you. Trust it. From open door to open door, trust each hallway in-between. You will never fail, you learn, you grow and not only do you win in the end, but you're also winning on the way!

Reflection

What do you know, like and trust about
yourself?

I know that I _____

_____

_____

_____

_____

_____

_____

_____

_____

_____

_____

8

LOVE LESSONS

I love LOVE! It really isn't as complicated as I made it. If you have ever been to a wedding, then chances are you are familiar with this passage of scripture referred to as the love chapter. "If I speak in the tongues of men or of angels, but do not have love, I am only a resounding gong or a clanging cymbal. 2 If I have the gift of prophecy and can fathom all mysteries and all knowledge, and if I have a faith that can move mountains, but do not have love, I am nothing. 3 If I give all I possess to the poor and give over my body to hardship that I may boast, but do not have love, I gain nothing. 4 Love is patient, love is kind. It does not envy, it does not boast, it is not proud. 5 It does not dishonor others, it is not self-seeking, it is not easily angered, it keeps no record of wrongs. 6 Love does not delight in evil but rejoices with the truth. 7 It always protects, always trusts, always hopes, always perseveres. 8 Love never fails. But where there are prophecies, they will cease; where there are tongues, they will be stilled; where there is knowledge, it will pass away. 9 For we know in part and we prophesy in part, 10 but when completeness comes, what is in part disappears. 11 When I was a child, I talked like a child, I thought like a child, I reasoned like a child. When I became a man, I put the ways of childhood behind me. 12 For now we see only a reflection as in a mirror; then we shall see face to face. Now I know in part; then I shall know fully, even as I am fully known.

"And now these three remain: faith, hope and love. But the greatest of these is love."

— Corinthians 13

I've heard this passage a lot in life, but for me, love was great expectations of how I saw my dad treat my mom. Him helping roll her hair or painting her toenails. Love was laughter and family. Love was my dad always making sure my sisters and I checked in on each other and said, "I love you." Love was a kiss on the forehead before bed and before you head out the door. Love was family dinners on Sundays and birthday parties all throughout the year. Love was my dad bringing me McDonald's for lunch on his days off and ginger ale and saltine crackers to my bedside when I was sick. I grew up surrounded by love. Love would be that and more as I got older.

Love would be listening when I talked, quality time and touch. Love would be hugs from my kids or leaving my toothbrush out on the sink. It's important to know what love is to you, but equally as important to know what love is NOT. I didn't know love was not always trying to fix it. Love is not trying to change someone. Love is not compromising your beliefs. It is also not asking the person you love to shrink. Love is not sacrificing joy to fit in. It is not playing small to cater to someone else's or even your own insecurities. I'm learning love lessons as life goes on. It keeps getting better and better!

Dear Daughter,

You will find a time when life will most certainly surprise you. Sometimes the surprises will thrill you and give you what feels like wings to fly! Cherish and embrace these times. Sometimes the surprises will feel like everything you think you knew, no longer makes sense. Even though you may not feel like it, try to embrace these times too. It is all part of your journey and designed to build trust in God and yourself. Change is inevitable and is meant to transform you. Remember the butterfly. When you are hurting, hug yourself and cry as much as you need to, talk to God and stay in His presence long enough to feel His response.

Don't let the fear of embarrassment or self-pride cause you to endure hardship alone. We grow better together. Find your community, your sister circle, your tribe. One that both supports and encourages as well as challenges you to be your very best! I put a lot of pressure on myself, trying to be perfect. I wasn't so concerned with getting it all right, as much as I was so scared of getting it wrong. The idea of messing up kept me up at night and stressed. I don't want that for you. I want you to know that your best is always good enough and that there is nothing you can't take to God. NOTHING! Take time to sit with yourself and learn to enjoy the quiet to hear your thoughts and feel your emotions. Embrace all of you, but at the same time, don't be afraid to let go of any parts that don't serve you.

If you find bitterness, seek to understand the hurt behind it and then take the steps to heal that hurt so you can let feelings like bitterness and resentment go. Affirm that you never fail. Even what may appear as failure will better you if you look for the lesson. So you never really fail. You learn and grow! I want you to be sure you laugh a lot. I've learned that it helps keep your heart warm.

Practice daily gratitude so that even on your toughest day, you know you've found some good you can focus on. Remember, "Thank you," makes room for more. Be sure of your voice, it always matters. Passionately pursue your purpose. It is the key to ultimate fulfillment. Your greatest joy will be using your gifts in service to others. This is why it is so important to love yourself FIRST. You have people that need your gifts. You always want to serve them out of your abundance. Be sure you fill your cup so you can serve out of the overflow.

You are not responsible for anyone else's happiness, no matter who may try to convince you differently. Likewise, remember you are as happy as you choose to be. Ask for help as much as you need to. It's ok to feel scared. Just never let it stop you from doing anything. Trust your intuition. It is a gift from God in the form of the Holy Spirit. Trust that feeling that says you are made for more and go after it! One of the greatest gifts is love, love more and allow yourself to be loved in return. Be compassionate and practice empathy.

Don't stay uncomfortable and shrink yourself to fit into spaces you've outgrown. You are already enough, don't ever apologize for being true to who you are. One day, as much as I wish I can prevent it, someone will hurt you. Allow yourself to process the hurt, to feel all the feels and to look for the lessons. After that, allow yourself to forgive. It will be one of the best gifts you'll ever give yourself. It's not about the other person, hurt people, hurt people. Forgiving doesn't mean you ever have to associate with the person again and it doesn't mean what they did wasn't wrong.

Forgiveness is a tool designed to free YOU! If you do not forgive others, our Father in heaven won't forgive you. I know this will be hard. Trust me, it was not easy for me to forgive some of my offenders. I held onto resentment for a long time. I remembered every offense so that I could see it coming the next time. I built walls of protection so I would never be hurt again. The harsh reality of that was I would never know the love I wanted with those walls there. It would be crowded out with resentment. I had flooded out good memories holding onto the offenses. True love and freedom were what I found on the other side of forgiveness. To experience the love I wanted, I needed to let go. So daughter, let go and let the wings of freedom carry you to love. Love for God, self and others. Know that you don't always have to speak to be heard.

Sometimes your silence will speak volumes by itself. Be purposeful about your higher habits. They will be reflected in your character. Remember, not everyone gets to have access to you, so be selective about the company you keep. Protect your peace and energy at all costs. You will get tired and feel weak along this journey. When you do, find rest and strength in the Lord. Take time to cater to your needs. Don't convince yourself that you have to keep going and do it all, be everything to everybody to prove your love, friendship, loyalty or strength. You do not have to always be the strong one to put on the mask and pretend you are ok when you're not. It's ok to exhale and take your cape off. Above all, seek God. He is always expecting you.

Love,
Mother

Dear Son(s),

Dear Son, be true to who you are. You don't have to pretend to be who they think you are or feel pressure to be anyone other than yourself. Honor your emotions. Know that it's ok to feel. Find a safe space where you can be vulnerable. Don't steal, and don't lie. Resist the urge to make someone pay for how someone else has hurt you. Respect yourself and remember you are made in the image of God. Be particular about who gets access to you and protect your peace and create good energy. Don't avoid confrontation at the cost of keeping things stuffed down and held in. Seek first to listen, then to understand and finally to have the wisdom of resolve. **Lifestyle Success Tip: Never seek to prove yourself to anyone.**

Don't let your ego keep you from the love your heart desires. Never let your pride keep you from apologizing. Look to learn your lessons the first time. Don't make excuses. Own your actions and stand in your truth. Through your mistakes you'll learn humility, grace and forgiveness. When the opportunity comes, extend that same grace to someone else.

The world will try to make you think that you aren't good enough. YOU ARE! There may come a day when you are scared and don't know what to do. It's ok, son, seek advice from someone that is where you're looking to go. Seek the face of God and His Word. He knows exactly what you need. Please cry when you need to. Trust me, that release will help add years to your life. Find a circle you trust, that will make you laugh and that you can be relaxed around. Find a woman that loves God more than you. Love her for who she is, not how she loves you, and respect her for the value she adds to your life Forgive and practice patience. Provide protection and security.

Remember the women in your life that did right by you. Honor your ancestors and the one that gave you life.

I want more than anything that you love God, fulfill His purpose in your life and that you do it full of peace, happiness and joy. Give God that same energy you give the game. Let the people know whose team you're on. Look for the people assigned to you. Surprise them with your compassion. Be kind to strangers. You never know when you're in the presence of an angel. Some people might mistake your strength for weakness, be careful about how you correct them. I pray you have the discernment to know when to let things go and when to stand your ground. You are valued, and your life matters!

Look after those entrusted to you. Choose quality over quantity. Stay present in the moments that matter the most. Make time for those who need you without expecting something in return. Be sure you never ask anyone to do something for you that you wouldn't do for them. Don't spend money you don't have or try to withdraw anything that wasn't deposited. Desire not only to please yourself but others. Smile often, laugh hard, love more and live your life with purpose, on purpose. Keep a grateful heart and a spirit that is open for more. You serve a God of abundance so never settle for good enough.

Don't tire of doing good. Know that it will always come back to you. Speak with both the confidence of the king you are and the King you serve. Embrace the journey and the change that is sure to come. Change will refine you and help you to step into your own. You do not have to know all the answers or have it all figured out. It's ok to need help and seek wise counsel. Hold onto all wisdom and let foolishness fall away. Don't hold onto your youth longer than what's good for you. When you feel like giving up, don't. You've got more to do, stay winning! *Lifestyle Success Tip: Keep your eyes clear and your nails clean.*

Love,
Mommy

4EVERMORE

There was a time I mourned a love I thought I would never know. I was told I listened to too many love songs and that I should get my head out of the clouds. Told I watch too many romances, and what I wanted didn't exist. I was told I was weak for leaving my marriage over a silly thing like love. I didn't take love lessons from Jill Scott or Beyoncé, but they do a good job of letting you know it's not all unicorns and rainbows. The last time I checked, Darius and Nina went through some things!

Yes, Love Jones is my favorite romance, and Love & Basketball got next! I'm here to tell you that LOVE is no silly thing, and I didn't leave my marriage because it wasn't a fairytale. I left it because it was a loveless lie. BUT LOVE, real love has the power to transform. It can make you do some silly things, but is by no means silly. Love is power, Love is God, Love is healing, Love is freeing. I wanted ALL. OF. THAT! I wanted friendship, authenticity, protection, consideration, security, companionship, and laughter. I have such a huge capacity to love, and like my daddy, I love hard! I wanted to love someone who thought what I had to say was worth listening to. Someone who loved me enough to tell the truth and be vulnerable enough to be themselves with me. I wanted someone to reach for my hand riding in the car and kiss me when they walked into the room. So yes, while I do love romance, I know there's more to it. I wanted to be able to argue and make up. I wanted to work out any differences TOGETHER. I wanted to be accepted on my worst day, celebrated on my best and valued and appreciated all in-between. I had faith in that kind of Love.

On my darkest days, I prayed God would change me, to help me to settle and be content without love. To survive not feeling loved or loving as big and hard as I always felt I was made to do. I could feel that love aching and bursting to get out. I had survived so many other painful experiences in my life because God had to carry the burden of pain or stepped in with the comfort only He can give. This, however, was a prayer God would never grant. So my heart ached instead for a love I didn't know. When I wanted to give up on love, God wouldn't let me. As you know, eventually I learned to love myself, which was good, but we don't serve a God of good enough.

When God made me, He knew just who He'd made me for. He knew who would need love as big as mine to match the big love they had to give. Imagine if I would have believed the doubters. What if I had just turned down my love songs when they came on the radio?

If God had answered my prayer not to care? I'm so grateful God didn't give me what I wanted. He knew what I needed more than I did, and He knew who he had for me. Love is everything! Love God, love yourself, and if you feel like it's in you and your heart is bursting at the seams then love someone else!

I started talking to my soulmate when my divorce was underway. The unpredictable timing led to rumors that he was the reason we were getting divorced, but that simply isn't true. Ex and I had gotten ourselves to that place well before. *Lifestyle Success Tip: Just because people feel entitled to an explanation does not mean you are obligated to give them one.*

Here's an interesting story about when I first saw "soulmate." He had walked into a training room I was onboarding in upon my return to corporate following the bankruptcy. He'd walked up to the instructor, and I had this feeling of, OH, I know him! That familiar feeling, only I couldn't recall from where. I looked at his badge for his name, Ricky Watkins. I drew a blank. He was no one I knew. It was very odd at the time, but I have no doubt now that my Spirit knew him because I had been created with him in mind.

I would see him in passing and buy the occasional chocolate bar when he was selling them for his son's school. I hated doing fundraisers. I'd always choose the buy-out option. I did love me some chocolate bars though. Anyway, he worked technical support for some of my orders. Unlike almost every other guy in the building, he was always respectful and always called me Mrs. "Ex's last name." The only conversation we'd had outside of troubleshooting tickets was whether I had any marriage tips to offer since he was engaged and about to be himself. I told him, "Don't lie."

I picked up that conversation two years later by asking

if he ever got married? I didn't see a ring, but that means little nowadays. With my marriage ending, I was wondering how my tip had worked out for him. He let me know they never got married, and they were no longer together. It hadn't worked out. I didn't really know him like that, but I was truly sorry to hear it. Before you knew it, we were sharing stories and discussing the complexities of relationships and why they prove to be some freakin' hard. The idea of two different people trying to become one. "What's your type?" I asked him. Let me add here that I don't know anything about how to pick up a guy, but apparently, that line will do the trick, lol. Soulmate was interested in why such a question, and although neither one of us was in a rush to get serious, it didn't seem we had any control of what would be our beginning of forever together.

I found out that soulmate and I had crossed paths before. We'd been working in the same building 13 years earlier yet never ran into each other. Here we were again together in a different building, on different floors. Almost like we'd been trying to catch up to each other. Soulmate was very cautious, convinced that after 18 years with a person, Ex and I were bound to work things out and call off the divorce. As a result, I would be friend-zoned for 4 months, which was cool because friendship was very important to me. I was being cautious too because I was in a good place loving myself now, using my voice and embracing freedom.

I didn't want anything or anyone to have me end up back where I was working so hard to get from. I was very clear about who I was and that any friendship and relationship we started would not change that. You get what you get, and I'm enough. Soulmate and I took time getting to know all about each other and enjoyed each other's company. It was he that assured me I was not my worst mistake. "That's just something you did. That's not who you are." In my self-love journey, I'd embraced that part of me, moved past the shame to accept it. This is what I'd done. This was who I was. That statement was freeing in that I could own my mistake without letting it define me. **Lifestyle Success Tip: A simple change in perspective can result in a significant change in perspective.**

Soulmate was certain that the trip to Disney World Ex and I were taking our kids on would be when I came back and told him we were back together. When I did not, we started officially dating, and it was an instant indescribable connection of souls.

Fact: I hated being called "girlfriend." It felt so "high school." Here I was, this grown woman with two kids, and now I was a "girlfriend." I had to shift my thinking and realize this was not starting over. I was starting again, and this time with lessons learned. I was introduced to his sons, my sons now, and it was instant love because they were an extension of him. I finally introduced him to my two children three months later. I asked my son what he thought of him. I would constantly check in with each of my kids, ask probing questions, try to make sure they were ok and see how they were processing the changes they were experiencing. He said, "I like him." when I asked, "why?" He said, "Because he makes you laugh." Aww, how cute, right? Well, it actually broke my heart. I was typically known for laughing a lot. Had I not been laughing? I had to sit with it and think about why that would be the thing that stood out to my 6-year-old son. That cloud of heaviness that came over me when I walked into my house had stolen my laughter. My children had not gotten the best of me, and that hurt my heart.

Although I didn't like being called a "girlfriend," I wasn't sure I wanted to be called a "wife" either. That hadn't turned out very well for me the first time around. I didn't want to ever be in a situation where someone felt obligated to stay with me or stuck because they'd taken a vow. I didn't want to be with anyone that didn't want to be with me. Rejection, neglect, and abandonment. These were all feelings I had felt and never wanted to feel again. I wanted to make it easy for him to leave me if he ever felt like it. I wanted to play it safe, to protect myself from experiencing that kind of rejection again. My logical mind thought, smart girl, that makes perfect sense.

So although I love LOVE and my new friendship and relationship was unlike anything I'd ever known in the best of ways, AND we could see only our futures together...getting married again became an internal struggle for me and spiritual conflict. I know what the bible says about divorce, what it says about marriage, and what it says about fornication. I knew who I wanted to be and how I wanted to show up for myself. This meant I had to yield, to once again surrender. This time I surrendered the fears and insecurities to allow myself to love completely and be loved completely in return.

I almost let the fear of failure cause me to run. I was guarded. I almost gave a second thought to what people might think about me moving on so soon. Only it wasn't soon. It had been a long time coming. I wrestled with fear and doubt that our love was too good to be true. I kept waiting for something to happen, to go wrong. At one point, I thought maybe I would die soon. Do you remember my bucket list? I thought maybe my life was coming to an end and God had seen fit to grant me this solid, the love I had always wanted. I know it sounds morbid, but it's my truth. I thought like that.

I asked my soulmate if he was scared too, having come out of an eight-year relationship with his sons mother. He said, "No, I can't love a little bit, if I'm going to love, I'm going all in! I'm not scared to take the "L." All the way in was all

I knew, but that was the part that scared me. All the way in was how I got lost, but now I had a new perspective. Don't be scared to take the "L." I want to pass that same sentiment on to you. Love all the way in, don't be scared to lose. I decided I would live in the moment and experience this amazing love for as long as it lasted. It still feels like it's just happening. It just IS. When people tell you marriage is work, they're talking about adjusting to each other's personality quirks, schedules, sleep patterns or preferences in how you raise the kids, things like that.

Love is not something you have to force. The love itself is not work. The love is why you get over all the other things that come up. Love is why I tolerate him scratching his throat (inside joke my sister Alma will get). Love is why he puts down his phone. Love is what says let it go, and sometimes love is what says let's talk this out.

Soulmate and I were married that same year, December 22, at the local courthouse. We received one single congratulations card. It was from Ex, asking for forgiveness and saying he forgave me and wished me well. Closure from years of what I've concluded was one mess of a very unhealthy marriage, but one to which I am so grateful for all of the lessons, preparation and my beautiful children it produced.

My love for my husband is not even close to what I thought was as good as love could get. Ten years and forever to go, I still have "I can't believe this is real" moments. I've found myself in tears recalling the person that did their best to convince me a love like this didn't exist. I know they did it from a place of love and that they were only telling me what they knew to be true. I would get sad that they never had the opportunity to experience a love like I now knew. You have to ask God what He has for YOU. What's for YOU is for YOU! Everyone won't get to experience it. They may not even believe it because they can't see past their own truth. I need you to stay open and ready to lean into everything God has for YOU!

Love is trust, communication, listening to learn, listening to understand. Love is laughing so hard your sides hurt at something only the two of you get. Love is a relationship. That's why prayer is so important. It's building a relationship with God. It's talking to Him and staying in His presence to listen to what He has to say. Caring about what is important to Him. My husband's patience with me is bar none. I mean, I get on my own nerves for him sometimes! Likewise, my patience with him, although if he leaves that bathroom drawer open one more time, I may have to publish a revision! Seriously though, we do have our days when we get on each other's nerves or say something without considering how it will make the other feel. The beauty of our friendship is we can call each other out and squash it before it becomes something neither one of us really wants. If you can keep that thought present, it will bless your life and your relationships. "What do I really want?"

I can tell you. I never want to argue, and I never want to hurt him. I never want to get on his nerves. Now do I and have I? Sure, but here's the work...we remember or maybe even remind each other of what we really want. Love will do that. Love will want to give the other person what they want. There's no time to let feelings fester and turn into a billion thoughts in the middle of the night that ends up being an hour-long movie reel instead of a 2-minute conversation. I know this happens because that's what I used to do the first time around. I used my first marriage as a reminder of what I did NOT want. I had to recall how it felt those nights. I really just wanted to reach over for a hug but instead let my pride keep me silent and up all night. Waiting to see if Ex would do it first. He never did.

There is no room for pride in your relationship. "What do I really want?" I want a hug. I want to not have us upset with each other. It used to make me feel needy to admit this. Now it just feels like me being true to who I am and what I want. My husband and I both have the same love language of Physical Touch, I'm a 10, and he's an 11. Let's just say making up is fun and leave it at that! Oh, and that lubricant keeps the party going! You're welcome. Back to my point (dang ADHD), you have to be honest about what you really want to give yourself the best chance of getting it. It's work to try to stay mad and be angry and remember that you're not talking. That silent treatment will do a job on your mental health! Let love lead you.

Accept each other's individual greatness. The key to doing that and having a successful relationship is to get to know each other first. There's no time to pretend during the dating phase. This is when you need to show up and be sure that they can handle all of you! There's no time for playing small or being insecure. You are enough. So love yourself enough to love all the way in! Love is knowing what you really want and believing you can have it. Love expands, love grows deep, love stretches wide. Love is going to have your back, love will support you, love will remind you of who and Whose you are when you forget it. **Lifestyle Success Tip: God is love, and Love never fails!**

Believe that you are worthy of love, deserving of all that you really want. Know that who is for you, is for you. Trust that all of your journey is preparing you and refining you for the love you are meant to experience. Love is loving yourself completely and bringing 100%. Love is saying sorry, love is owning when you're wrong and not feeling the need to prove when you're right.

"If an angel came down to me
Ask what I would do differently
I would say nothing you see
I love someone truly."

—If Tonight is My Last by Laura Izibor

Dear Love,

I believe with all of my soul, my heart was made to love you. God knew just what we needed when He created us to complement each other so well. You are the perfect fit! Thank you for embracing ALL of me so tightly. Your heart is so willing to search, to find the good in everyone. It drives me crazy, but it's one of the things I love most about you. So many things to love about you! I love you for being consistent and true to who you are. It provides me with security. I love you for holding my hand and guiding me, for placing me on the inside when we walk. I feel safe. I love you for paying close enough attention to me to know when I'm 'off' and genuinely caring what's wrong. I feel seen. I love how you've helped me navigate through my "baggage" with such patience and understanding. I feel special. I love your confidence, intelligence and eagerness to grow in knowledge. I love how you fill in wherever needed without being asked. I love that we get each other's annoyances and upsets. You help me to show up better. I love that telling each other how much we appreciate each other never gets old. I love that you still call to check on me and ask if I'm ok. I love our car rides and conversations and our evening walks holding hands. I love that you can tell if I'll like something or not, and I can trust you to be right. We've taken time to get to know each other so well. I love that I can still make you blush and that you still give me butterflies. We make an amazing team. I love our family! I love how attentive you are to detail. It shows in all you do. I love that you're always up for a challenge and down for whatever my spontaneity brings. We're still keeping each other young. I love that I never have to fake a headache and that you take the time to know me. I feel fortunate. I love that you find joy in the little things and choose happy for yourself. I love that you can laugh at yourself and my corny jokes. You get me. You are so wonderful, and I'm not just saying that, although I do tell you a lot. I am blessed. I love that you still pull me close. I feel wanted. I love that you are your own person. I feel proud. I love your love for music. Sneakers, not so much, but you do look hella good in them! I love that you love reading and traveling too! We go so good together. Thank you, love, for letting me know you're proud of me, for reminding me I can do anything I put my mind to. Thank you for assuring me of your love with your actions. It's fascinating, I don't feel like our love is anything we're doing, but I still want to let you know I appreciate it and YOU! I tell you so very often. I love loving you because I really do. Your heartbeat will forever be my favorite song on the soundtrack to my life. Thank you, love, for trusting me to love you and loving me "all the way in." I still see YOU.

I love you 4EVERMORE,
Jamie

Reflection

What are your greatest love lessons?
How have they impacted how you love?

My greatest love lessons are _____

_____

_____

_____

_____

_____

_____

_____

_____

_____

9

PURSUING PURPOSE

Purpose is the reason we are here! Purpose is where you find ultimate fulfillment. Purpose is why I'm writing this book. You are equipped with the gifts you need to fulfill the purpose you were created for. Even the pain has meaning! God turned my pain into purpose! Isn't that absolutely amazing?! As you've read, I spent a lot of time chasing what I told myself would fulfill me. What I thought I needed from other people. When God had placed everything I needed within me for both Himself and others.

If anyone ever tells me they've found their purpose and it doesn't involve service to others, I suggest they keep looking. We were not meant to do this life alone. Thus my motto "We grow better together!" Seek God for direction, read His word and listen for His Spirit to guide you. It was when I surrendered trying to "fix it" and do things my way that I saw God moving. I was able to see that I had been in my way. It was then I heard Him remind me I was fearfully and wonderfully made. I was able to look inward and find love for myself and allow the Spirit to guide me out of the darkest place of my life. God's love for me would remind me of Whose I was and that I was created with purpose. Before I was affirming I was enough, God determined it. I had to love myself enough to accept it as my truth. This is why I advocate for self-love first. If you do not love yourself, you'll struggle to believe you are who God says you are. You'll struggle to truly love others too. You will attract an unhealthy "love".

Unfortunately, it can result in finding yourself in a relationship like I did where hurt people, hurt people. God doesn't want that for you, and neither do I. Love yourself enough to believe God created you with a purpose you're meant to fulfill.

The beauty of being born with our gifts and created with purpose is that it's a built-in, full-proof plan. You may be looking for your purpose right now. You need only look within. There are gifts you have in you that someone needs. You may already know what they are, or maybe you have yet to identify them, know they are there. I have known for a long time my gifts were service, giving, discernment and encouragement. I've taken several spiritual gifts assessments, and they all come back the same. But before any tests, I knew what brought me joy. I love helping people. When I was little, I found joy in making homemade cards and giving people gifts. I was your hype girl, the one that was going to let you know you could do it and be there to encourage you, be it with an audible cheer or a silent hug. The many roles I dreamed of playing through the years were always some type of service, teacher, nurse, counselor, wife and mother.

You may be thinking about your life now and how your gifts are showing up. It's not enough to know them though. You have to be purposeful about using them and with the right motives. I sat on my gifts for a long time, and I got in my way about not being good enough, qualified, worthy or deserving. The epiphany was, it wasn't about me. My gifts, just like those homemade cards when I was little, were for someone else. If you're reading this, then that someone else is YOU. Just like me, you have something someone else is waiting for. Something that will help them and remind them there is a good side.

16 SPIRITUAL GIFTS LIST

(Romans 12, Ephesians 4 & Corinthians 12)
- Administration / Ruling
- Apostleship / Pioneering
- Discernment
- Encouraging / Exhorting
- Evangelism
- Faith
- Giving
- Hospitality
- Knowledge
- Leadership
- Pastor / Shepherding
- Prophecy / Perceiving
- Teaching
- Serving / Ministry
- Showing Mercy
- Wisdom

You are equipped with everything you need to fulfill your God-given purpose. If you think back, in some way, shape or form, you have been using your gifts. Maybe it's knowledge or wisdom. Maybe you have the gift of hospitality. I have always used my gifts in some capacity, and as I aligned myself with God's will for my life, I could feel there was more I should be doing with them. Do you ever feel like something's missing that you can't quite put your finger on? Like there has to be more to life? Good news! There is, Sis, and seeking God and purpose will lead you to it.

When I started my self-love journey, it was about escaping the hurt and pain of despair and disappointment. It was almost an act of defiance that if Ex wasn't going to love me, like everything else I wanted done, I would have to do it myself! That quickly shifted to seeking God because I didn't know where to start. What I did know was that God was love. Remember, I started out buying Old Navy items of the week, which was nice and brought some temporary satisfaction. But it wasn't enough to fill the void and feelings that I wasn't enough and was too hard to love. There was still something missing. God had not made any mistakes with me, everything I was feeling was real, but I wasn't meant to stay in that place. It was so that I could grow from that place and step further into my purpose.

It's moments like that that allow me to say with confidence, where you are right now, is not where you're meant to stay. You are meant to look for the lesson, remember who and Whose you are and love yourself on your journey through that hallway. I'm not assuming you're in a place you don't want to be. I'm sharing that life is a continuous journey. So if you are in a place you would rather not stay, don't worry, you won't. Not as long as you look for the lessons, embrace the change they will bring, remember who you are, you are enough and equipped, and you are a child of the most high God. If you are somewhere you would rather stay, you won't. That's not a bad thing. It's just that you are not designed to settle. You are meant to grow and elevate. There is always something you can learn and always something that you can be better at. **Lifestyle Success Tip: You are enough, equipped and empowered for purpose!**

Even when I found myself choosing happy and it seemed like life was genuinely good, I could not settle. God said there was more. My self-love journey led me to my soulmate. You may just find what you need the moment you stop looking for what you want. Pursue purpose, and everything you need will find you. **Lifestyle Success Tip: Be grateful, but don't miss out on your greater holding so tightly to your good!**

CREATE THE LIFE YOU WANT

So what does pursuing purpose look like? I'm going to give you a simple answer. Whatever you want. I am mindful and intentional about enjoying my journey and, come what may, embracing that I get to create the life I want. Yes, God orders my steps, but He also promises to give me the desires of my heart. You'll see that the two align quite nicely.

Lifestyle Success Tip: Check your heart's desires!

I love to travel, and so my family and I do that as often as we can. I love to laugh, smile, love and LIVE. It is so important to take the time for the things that bring you joy. My husband surprised me for my 40th birthday with an intimate dinner with some of my closest friends and family.

He topped that surprise by gifting me a trip to Paris. Tickets and Rosetta Stone for French (no excuse why I'm not fluent by now). Though traveling the world had been something I'd said I wanted, and I'd been on about eight cruises by then, it had never occurred to me Paris was an option. I had limited myself to what I knew I could obtain. Enjoying your journey will look like removing the limits on what you think it is going to look like. Not boxing in your vision and opening your mind up to abundance, to new places, new people and new things. It is going to require that shift in perspective, a new growth mindset. We've been back to Paris since that first trip and will eventually own a place to live there. When I say that to some people, they chuckle. Like a "yeah right." I used to be that same person that couldn't see past what I knew. My journey has taught me that just because I haven't experienced something doesn't mean it doesn't exist or can't be done. *Lifestyle Success Tip: Be careful not to let people project their limited beliefs and fears onto you. Assess if maybe you already have.*

The only limit is the one you put on yourself. That same little girl that couldn't see past getting married and buying a house, was now planning to live in Paris, France. The twenty-something-year-old woman who didn't think her voice mattered was speaking to women worldwide and now writing her first book. My point to you is to dare to believe there is greater in you. Let go of limiting beliefs and childhood conditioning.

If you are like me, then you can finish this statement...

"When we get inside this store...."

Yup, you got it!

"YOU BETTER NOT ASK ME FOR NOTHIN'!"

We've been conditioned to settle for less. Taught to be happy with what we have and not to ask for more. I'm sure that was not our parent(s) intent, but the narrative took root and grew just the same. If you have ever settled for something under the notion that it could be worse, I want to challenge you to think instead that it could be BETTER! I was able to move beyond my limits by reading a very popular self-help book. One line of the whole book changed my life in such a way I dared to believe beyond what I could see! That one line was, "Your dream doesn't have an expiration date." That's it. That is the line. It's that line that propelled me toward my purpose. I had a dream to serve others and travel. I had a dream to retire from corporate and open a nail salon, common community space, home for girls…the dreams changed over the years, but the purpose was always the same. To use my gifts to service others. I won't quote you that line since it's been taken, but I will tell you that if you want to do it, don't let anyone tell you that you can't! By anyone, I mean YOU! I had limited myself over the years.

I disqualified myself because I didn't finish college, had gotten divorced, and had filed for bankruptcy. I told myself I was too old, and it was too late, I wasn't good enough. Focused all my energy on what I didn't have or the heavy parts of my journey. My self-love journey and living happily ever after was continuous change and growth. I started embracing the excitement of where God would lead me next. Now, God was letting me know it was time for a new season, regardless of resources or any other excuse I had tried to convince myself was valid. It was time to MOVE! I felt that deep in my spirit. I talked to my husband about it on Paradise Beach in the Bahamas, one of the stops on the cruise we took my daughter on for her Sweet 16. I let him know I had to do something. I was only sure about two things at the time.

1. I wanted to impact the lives of women.
2. I wanted to be able to do that from wherever I was in the world.

I had a purpose to live. YOU have a purpose to live. It is not a single destination. It is a lifestyle. I did not have a lot of money at my disposal to invest, but I chose this time to focus on what I did have. I was so excited I couldn't sleep for weeks. I was so full of ideas, and the purpose in my belly was ready to be birthed. I did what I could with what I had, and in 3 months, I had launched mypeaceofhappy.com, a lifestyle blog at the time, encouraging women in health and fitness, personal growth, relationship, and travel.

When I was reminded that my dream had no expiration date, my vision was bigger than what I thought I was equipped to do, but I was also reminded I serve an even BIGGER God! All I had was a desire to fulfill my purpose and what I wanted it to look like. Shifting my focus from everything I didn't have that I thought I needed, to doing what I could with what I had. Fast forward two years, I would take my husband on a two-week trip to Aruba for his birthday. Now mypeaceofhappy.com was an LLC and Trademarked as the coaching, consulting, podcasting, speaking and community brand you know today. Why am I going into these details? Because I want you to see that you can start small and work with what you have. Purpose, faith and an idea you can make a reality. Your gifts will make room for you. I get to help and empower women to live their life with purpose, and I get to do it from wherever I am! This is just the beginning of all God has shown me. It started with believing God's purpose for my life had not expired, trusting the vision, and setting the goals to create it.

Lifestyle Success Tip: You get to create the life you want!

Trust me when I tell you that you have everything you need. Dare to believe in the greater dream and vision God has placed on your heart. God has shown me so clearly that I'm speaking on stages and signing my books. I still haven't seen those stages, but I know they are coming, and well, here you are reading my first book! Getting out of your head and out of your way will take effort. Some days will be more challenging than others. It is hard work, but faith without works is dead. Start scared if you have to. Just START!

It took me 3 years to finally start writing this book. I journaled for almost two years straight that I was a best-selling author but never picked up my pen to write. Why? I was scared. It was easier to just keep saying I had a book in me and that I'd be a best-selling author. I got in my head about it. What would happen if I started writing and it wasn't a book after all? What if it was a book and it wasn't a best-seller? I got in my way. I'm sorry it took me so long to get this to you. I made it about me when it was about sharing my story to help someone else. You're sitting on your gifts! Get up off your vision! *Lifestyle Success Tip: Your story and gifts aren't for you. Someone is waiting that needs what you have.*

My husband and I recently took our whole family back to Aruba, one of our favorite places and embraced the blessing of being able to do so. It was our first time bringing our children with us. "One Happy Island" is their motto, and it truly is. The warmth of the sun and the joy of our children getting to experience it. I don't know that we would have ever taken them out of school for two weeks to do this, but with the pandemic having made virtual classes an option now available to us, we took advantage of the opportunity. I encourage you to take full advantage of the opportunities that become available to you and know also, that you can create them yourself.

My smile, happiness, and peace are all results of living my peace of happy and living my life with purpose. I want you to also know you have options. Replace scarcity with abundance and limits with options. Your reality is going to be whatever you believe it can be. Create the life you want!

GREATER

I've been picking a word of intention since I started My Peace of Happy. In 2019 it was "Significant." In 2020, it was "Impact," and for 2021, it is "GREATER"! I didn't know what would come of the blog in 2019, but I intended to not just put information on the internet. I wanted it to be significant. I wanted organic growth, genuine connections, and to make a difference in the lives of the women in the community. I remembered this quote from Oprah Winfrey that said, "The key to realizing a dream is to focus not on success but on significance - and then even the small steps and little victories along your path will take on greater meaning."

I showed up every single day of 2019 and shared simple yet significant posts, stories, blogs and formed amazing community connections with amazing women. By 2020, I knew that was not enough. Significant was good, but I wanted to do more. I wanted to make an impact! I shared with my coach, who I hired at the launch of My Peace of Happy, to hold me accountable to my purpose. To help keep me from getting in my way, down the rabbit hole of overwhelm and overthinking. This is an example of being true to yourself. I know myself, and I know that I can delay myself by overthinking and second-guessing if given the chance.

So I asked for help and what a great help it was! By 2020 I knew the vision was even bigger. I was made to make a bigger impact. I was to speak, write books, and coach women in self-love to help them find their Peace of Happy (purpose), like I had found mine. My coach and I talked about what that would look like and planned out the year full of events that would support it. A video series of me speaking to small groups of women who would share their stories and experiences. "We grow better together" is the motto because I believe we can learn a lot from each other's stories and there is a significant impact in knowing you are not alone. Other women have gone through or are going through similar experiences, we are all very different, yet very much the same. We want to be seen, heard and loved. We planned out 6 events, 5 small ones and a larger workshop event. I think you can guess what happened to those 2020 plans, but I'll tell you anyway...a global pandemic happened! On fire with great expectations for 2020, I looked for the lesson. Impact! It wasn't a question now of WHEN, but of WHAT. What could I do now to create an impact? I went onto Instagram and searched for coaches. I was immediately drawn to an African-American woman whose profile read, "The Coaches Coach." The first video I clicked on was on sharing your story and a free upcoming workshop on how to become a life coach in 2020. Ok, I see you, God! I registered right away!

Lifestyle Success Tip: Stop saying what you're going to do "one day" and decide TODAY is that day!

Previously, I shared with my business coach about my concerns with not having a degree or what qualifications were required for becoming a coach. Exactly...getting in my head about it. I'm glad you can recognize it now when you see it. He had been assuring me I was already doing it, and one of my close friends had recently shared her testimony with me and reminded me I was already equipped with my gifts to impact lives. So when I heard, no certification was needed during the workshop, that your experience had qualified you, and the framework she shared would give me the directions on how to get to where I was going, I knew it had been a divine appointment orchestrated by God.

Three months later, I was establishing my LLC, filing my Trademark and obtaining my coaching certification, though not required, it is nice to have. You get to choose to look at the circumstances or past them! *Lifestyle Success Tip: Plans change: reset, adjust and keep moving forward.*

God had given me an idea for a program while in the 30-Day Life Coach Bootcamp. During my mentorship and certification course, when it came time to build out my program, I would question if that idea was a good one. I doubted myself and therefore doubted God. I took a suggestion to change it. Maybe, I wasn't ready, maybe it was too much to take on. I went on to sign up for two more programs, run several workshops and a virtual summit instead, all in 2020. I set out to have 6 paying clients by the end of the year. I got my sixth one on 12/31/20. I wish now I would have said at least 25 paying clients. I still wasn't thinking BIG enough. Don't you do that! Dream BIGGER!

When 2021 came, like most people I knew, there were great expectations that it had to be better than 2020! Everyone hoping "outside" would stay open, glad to get a new administration in the white house and just thankful that we had made it when so many lives sadly had not. My family and I had been blessed, my husband and I were both able to work at home, and I had been able to officially launch my business. During a lot of uncertainty and anxious times, God had shown me not even a global pandemic could stop what He had purposed me to do.

I still wasn't speaking, had not written my book or launched the program He had given me, but I was coaching. I was at least doing something. When it came to my 2021 word, I first thought of purpose, but it didn't stick, then thought maybe faithfulness, stay faithful to the vision God gave me. That didn't stick either. Then it came to me as I was expressing how 2020 had not been all bad, and I was looking forward to what God would do in 2021. "GREATER!" that's what came through loud and clear. I tried to imagine what greater would look like. Would it be 5 figure months in my coaching business, would I make enough to start building my team, how would greater manifest in my life? By April, good ole anxiety came back to visit. I questioned God because we're cool like that, He doesn't get easily offended…is GREATER still coming? I was sure I'd heard it right, "GREATER!" Then it came through. It sounded like my mom's voice, saying, "Don't ask me for anything else until you do what I told you to do!" Ouch, but I got it. I had to put myself in a timeout and reflect on what I had been doing instead. **Lifestyle Success Tip: Believing doesn't mean you'll never doubt. Just don't go down the rabbit hole.**

My lack of obedience was delaying my GREATER. Not just mine, but I was delaying someone else's breakthrough. I enrolled in a speaking program and hired an author coach. No lie, when I tell you, it was like God said, "FINALLY!" and opened the floodgates. To give you an idea of what I mean, I went from 1830+ followers to almost 6000 in three weeks. I would love to say it was one of my coaching videos, but it wasn't, and I know why…God wanted to show me it's not about me. It's Him, and He can use anything He chooses. So a video I shared giving my son his first car drove the traffic and because I was consistent in showing up, I had tons of valuable content waiting for lives I was meant to impact. I want YOU to think about how you're showing up. What has God told you that you're in your head and in your way about? Sis, get it done! It can be delaying your GREATER. Dare to believe that if God gave you the vision, He will see it through. You just have to do your part. The breakthroughs and next-level growth this writing experience has provided, it became clear that this was never about the book. It was about the process of writing the book, the obedience, the breakthroughs, and the transformation. That is what I believe this book will be for you as well. I hope that you can learn from my lessons and tips something that will cause the purpose within you to stir. That you do not sit on your gifts and the vision God gave you.

Dear God,

Forgive me for whoever's breakthrough I delayed by sitting on the vision You gave me. Thank You for Your favor and Your promises. Thank You for spoiling me with Your love and a love so true. Thank You for saving a sinner like me and Your Holy Spirit residing in me to help me every day to be better. To be more like You, to not lean to my own understanding, but acknowledge You. Your grace and mercy guide me, protect me, and I am so grateful. I know that I can do nothing without You, but all things through You. Please help me to remain in You and be obedient to Your will and purpose for my life.

Love Your daughter,
Jamie

Reflection

What will you do today to passionately
pursue your purpose?

I will passionately pursue my purpose by _____

_____

_____

_____

_____

_____

_____

_____

_____

_____

_____

10

LIFESTYLE SUCCESS

Lifestyle Success is an accumulation of all of the higher habits you keep. Self-love, mindset shifts, purpose, passion, your emotional, mental and physical well-being. Lifestyle Success isn't just the house and trips to Aruba and Paris, although that can be part of it. Lifestyle Success is self-love, self-care and how you show up for others. It is all you do which becomes who you are. The random acts of kindness, honoring your boundaries, aligning with your core values. Lifestyle Success is something that I coach my soulmate clients through to find that work-life balance so many women are looking for. Lifestyle Success is resting when you need to and then hitting that grind when you know that's what it will take to get it done. It is choosing happy and realizing that you can control a whole lot more than this world would have you to believe. It's deciding your vibe and your tribe.

Lifestyle success is passionately pursuing your purpose and looking for the people that are assigned to you. Some people will be a service to you, others for you to service. People are watching you, they may not say anything, but they are watching you to see if you are true to who you say you are. They want to know if you are authentic. Living your life with purpose and Lifestyle Success will show others they can do it too. Living out loud, flaws and all will encourage the woman that is scared to get it wrong. It will inspire that woman that thinks she's her worst mistake. Lifestyle Success will show that woman that there is redemption after the fall. Walking in the grace and mercy of God, Lifestyle Success is being intentional about defining your happiness, how you carry yourself, how you speak to yourself and others. Lifestyle Success is a journey, a never-ending process of choosing greater. It won't be over until you hear, "Well done, my good and faithful servant."

Lifestyle success is knowing that you not only win in the end but that you're winning along the way. It's making time to celebrate the small wins just as much as the big ones. Lifestyle Success is having the confidence to do it scared and know that you never fail. You learn, you grow, you get better!

Lifestyle Success is what I want for YOU! It is what I hope that you want for yourself. Fully embrace your story and this one life you get. Be determined to be your very BEST self for both yourself and those around you. You'll find out Lifestyle Success is contagious! People will ask you how you do what you do. Community over competition, teach what you know, share and always point to the true source, give God the glory. Know that His plan is always better than yours and that if you seek Him first, He will give you the desires of your heart. Lifestyle Success is accepting that everything in your life is happening for you to become who you are purposed to be. It is designed to create joy, peace, perseverance, kindness, goodness, faithfulness, gentleness, and self-control in you.

"But the fruit of the Spirit is love, joy, peace, forbearance, kindness, goodness, faithfulness, gentleness and self-control. Against such things there is no law."

—Galatians 5:22-23

Lifestyle Success is loving and taking care of your body. It is trusting God first and then yourself. Lifestyle Success is cultivating your circle and knowing you are enough. It is surrendering the fear, the perfectionism, running on empty and burning yourself out. All those things that no longer serve you. Lifestyle Success is being open to opportunities that challenge you and creating possibilities. It is accepting the truth, even when it hurts and processing your pain in your darkest days. Lifestyle Success is smiling in the rain because you know the waters are cleansing and bringing forth a bloom.

Lifestyle Success is in everything you do. It's comfy socks or no socks at all. It is being free to be. It is asking for help. It is being there for someone like someone was there for you. Lifestyle Success is paying it forward. It is allowing yourself to imagine you can have what you want and daring to dream BIGGER. It is believing good things can happen to you and you are deserving of the life you want. Lifestyle Success is forgiving and letting go. It is no longer letting your voice be silenced. Lifestyle Success is creating space and not trying to fit in. It is a mani-pedi on a Summer day and enjoying the breeze on a Fall afternoon.

Lifestyle Success is whatever makes your heart and soul joyful and keeps your mind at peace. It is being willing to lean into the vision God gave you for your life. It is trusting that all things work together for the good of those who love Him. Lifestyle Success is not self-sabotaging and settling for less than the abundant life God has for you. Lifestyle Success is love, family and friends that support you and build you up. It is not overthinking your ability but believing in your success. Lifestyle Success is knowing you can actually have Lifestyle Success! It is not letting your limiting beliefs stop you from creating the life you REALLY WANT!

GET EXCITED!

The journey of writing this book and becoming a best-selling author has been such an encouragement. I realize the vision God gave me is so much bigger than I imagined. Although it took me three years, I'm finally here. I'm so glad He never stopped nudging me. Obedience was definitely the key to writing this book. I wasn't finally ready. I was no better a writer than when He first showed me the vision. I was no more confident in myself to complete it. But I decided to do it scared, to be obedient, and my next step was to get help. This journey has given me a greater appreciation of my past, present and the ability to see a greater future.

I hope that something you've read has inspired you to embrace and accept your past, your present and get excited about your future! There is GREATER in store. I've started therapy through the course of writing this book, I realized that I'd been fast-forwarding through my emotions of grief, hurt and pain. While I do encourage you to keep moving forward, I also encourage you to take the time you need to process your emotions. Seek to better understand where they may stem from, and in doing so, you'll better understand yourself.

I want you to be able to look for and grow from all the

lessons you are meant to get out of your current season and then get excited about what is to come. Get excited about the change even though it's going to be difficult sometimes. Get excited about the mindset shift that takes place when you start believing you are just getting started. There is so much more for you! Your journey of self-love, happiness, and purpose will cleanse you, refine you, and make you better for your next open door. Get excited about those things that may now make you uncomfortable. I was not a writer. This was a challenging writing journey for me to have to gather my thoughts enough to type them out. Though it's been a challenge, I had to embrace it to get the change required for the next level of greater God promised me. Amen. I'm so proud of myself that I was brave enough to do it even when I was scared, to ask for help, to acknowledge what I didn't know, and get the help I needed to bring this vision to life. I celebrate myself, so you can see what that looks like and be purposeful about celebrating yourself as well! You're still standing Sis. You're winning! **Lifestyle Success Tip: Get excited and celebrate yourself!!!**

Dear YOU (reader),

Thank you for sharing this space with me and being a part of my journey. You were assigned to me, and now that we've connected through this experience, I look forward with great excitement for whatever God will do in your life! I'm not ready for us to part yet. It would mean so much to me if you let me know what you took away from reading my story and wrote a review. I know that this was not just for me, but for YOU too! Let's stay connected.

I hope you've benefited from the reflections and that the Lifestyle Success Tips bring a new sense of mindfulness in your everyday life. I'll leave you with a bonus kick-starter, a few steps I've taken myself. Sharing is caring, and we grow better together! Be encouraged, be inspired, be elevated to your next level of GREATER! Love yourself enough to embrace your process and enjoy your journey of Happily Ever After and Lifestyle Success!

Peace & Happy,
Jamie

10 Steps to
Self-Love, Happiness & Purpose

1 - Embrace Your Story

In the words of Tony Robbins, Life is happening FOR you! Everything that has happened up till this very moment has been to grow you, teach you and strengthen you. You're still standing, you survived, and your best is yet to come!

Whatever hurt, guilt, shame, anger or unforgiveness you may identify with your story, let it go. Embrace ALL of your story to help prepare you for your purpose.

Reflection:

How can your story help someone else?

2 - Identify Your Gifts

Do you ever feel like you don't have what it takes? I have good news! You were born equipped with everything you need to fulfill your purpose.

This should excite you! You no longer have to wrestle with not feeling good enough or feeling like you don't belong. Your gifts have not only equipped you, but they will make room for you.

Try This:

Be intentional about identifying your gifts and putting them to good service.

3 - Establish Your Core Values

In short, your core values are what are most important to you in life. They are the beliefs that help guide your thoughts, words and actions. Your core values will serve as a guide to help you in your everyday decision-making.

You will find that you are less likely to overcommit and more likely to feel good about your time spent doing the things you find meaningful. Core values help you to prioritize and better align yourself with your purpose.

Reflection:

What are your top 5 Core Values?

4 - Pursue Your Purpose

You were created with a purpose only you can fulfill. If you can identify with feeling like there has to be more to life or that you are made for more, it's because there is, and you are!

Seek to discover your purpose, passionately pursue why you are here. The peace, happiness, and fulfillment found in living your life's purpose is indescribable, and the journey is liberating!

Reflection:

How can you passionately pursue your life's purpose?

5 - Shift Your Mindset

Pursuing your purpose is a journey that will require a mindset shift. That will mean believing that you are unstoppable! It means knowing that fulfilling your purpose is your destiny and not an optional pursuit.

Shift your mindset from a fixed mindset to a growth mindset. This will allow you to be open to new opportunities and flexible to change. It will help you see the positive in every situation and keep moving forward no matter what!

The mind is so powerful. What you think, you become. Be purposeful about developing a growth mindset. Shift your thoughts to support the vision you have for living your life with purpose.

Reflection:

What do you need to change your mind about?

6 - Courageous Confidence

You will inevitably have to face your fears. Fear of what others will say or think, fear of failure, and maybe even fear of success. Overcoming your fears will take courageous confidence. It will mean being afraid and doing it when you are uncertain of what the outcome will be. Confidence is like a muscle that has to be exercised. The more you take the chance and push past your fears, the more confidence you will gain in knowing that you can do it.

Reflection:
What area of your life can you exercise courageous confidence in?

7 - Set Boundaries

When you decide to be intentional about living your life's purpose, it will take dedication and commitment. It may require long days and late nights. Allow yourself to set boundaries for yourself and others with regard to you.

Setting boundaries may look like saying "no" and not feeling guilty about it. Making time to prioritize self-care means you may need to communicate the importance to your children or spouse. Time blocking your schedule and creating a routine that will allow you time to journal, meditate and create as it relates to your self-care and further defining your purpose.

Reflection:
Where can you set boundaries to help you step further into your purpose?

8 - Cultivate Your Circle

The company we keep can influence us for the better or worse. I want to note that your circle of influence is not limited to people. Your circle of influence can include social media feeds as well. It is so important to cultivate your circle of influence to one that will serve you well.

Assess if your circle(s) supports your core values. Do they not only support you, but challenge you to be the best version of yourself? You may find that you have to unfollow, unfriend or block some content or "friends" to grow and progress on your journey to defining your purpose. Some courageous conversations may be necessary to do what is best for you and where your purpose is leading you.

Consider this:

Be encouraged that pulling up the weeds makes room for the flowers to grow!

9 - Plan Your Purpose Path

Write the vision, make it plain. Goal setting is an essential part of having a plan. Keep in mind that plans change, and we should expect to adapt and adjust. That, however, does not mean you do not set out with your plans and set goals to support them.

Of course, I am a fan of prayer and S.M.A.R.T

(Specific, Measurable, Achievable, Relevant and Time-bound) goals. Setting S.M.A.R.T goals will help you to actively track your progress and bring ·your plans and purpose closer to reality.

Try this:
Write at least one S.M.A.R.T goal you want to achieve over the next couple of weeks.

10 - Be Accountable

You are responsible for living out the purpose for which you were created. What are you doing with your gifts? Personal accountability is needed in this space. As much as you may like to put the responsibility on others, you must own and hold yourself accountable for what you do with your gifts, talents, time, and ultimately your purpose. Reclaim the power you have to create the life you want for yourself. Hire a life coach (I am here to help), get a mentor or accountability partner you can trust.

JOIN THE LIFESTYLE SUCCESS ACADEMY

I'll help you embrace self-love and gain clarity on your purpose so you can achieve lifestyle success.

Jamie Watkins

Get Excited About...

1. My Signature Lifestyle Success Strategy
2. Breaking through limiting beliefs
3. Overcoming overwhelm and perfectionism
4. Moving beyond self-doubt and insecurities
5. Gaining clarity on your purpose and vision
6. Growing better together with like-minded women

JOIN US NOW!

Visit mypeaceofhappy.com/coaching

ABOUT THE AUTHOR

Faith-based best-selling author, certified life coach, impact speaker, podcaster and entrepreneur Jamie Watkins wants women everywhere to embrace their stories, stand confidently in their truths and create the lives they want! Often called the "Happiness Coach," she is the founder of My Peace of Happy, a coaching, consulting and community brand dedicated to uplifting others. Jamie is known for her infectious smile, positive energy, down-to-earth approach and keen ability to connect with a powerful message rooted in self-acceptance, empower-ment and living with purpose.

By sharing her own journey from grief, heartache and pain to love, peace and purpose, Jamie proves that we are not alone in our struggles. As a recovering perfectionist and planning control freak, she understands what it's like to be "stuck" trying to control the uncontrollable and fix the unfixable. To pave the way for better days, she helps others brave the beauty of sweet surrender, embrace the freedom of forgiveness and find greater happiness in all areas of life.

Jamie is a proud "Jersey Girl" who currently resides

in Pennsylvania with her husband, four children and a toy poodle named Reesie Cup. She loves love, Jesus, community, traveling, reading, photography, butterflies and the warmth of the sun.

Jamie believes that through shared experiences, we can all learn to care more today than we did yesterday about ourselves, our dreams, our purposes and mankind. And because we grow better together, Jamie welcomes new connections through networking and social media.

"Most of all, I remember the music and the nostalgia that comes back when I hear a song from the soundtrack of my life."

Scan to download free playlist

Made in USA - North Chelmsford, MA
1289596_9781636160627
11.12.2021 0733